Many evangelism books are like fad diets—they serve up a faith-sharing method that you work hard to put into practice but give up on when things get tough. *Always Going*, however, points readers to a lasting lifestyle change in which the gospel spills out naturally, in both word and deed. This book kicks guilt to the curb, freeing and equipping Christians to joyfully live out their mission to populate God's eternal kingdom by conversationally sharing the good news in their circles of influence. I guarantee there's no better way to live!

Greg Stier | Founder and visionary of Dare 2 Share Ministries

Andrew Steier has written a powerful book about the value of living with an outward focus as we are *Always Going*. He has framed evangelism in a developmental way that will help every person. You will enjoy the illustrations and the easy-to-read format while learning simple ways to improve your ability to share Christ with those God brings into your life. I highly commend this book to you!

Dr. Dann Spader | Founder of Sonlife Ministries and Concentric Global; author of *4 Chair Discipling* and *Live Like Jesus*

Always Going crosses the spectrum from removing the pressure of sharing your faith to compelling you to speak up! Andrew Steier engages your heart and mind through relatable stories to help you better understand the gospel and provides practical next steps to share it with others. Change your mindset about evangelism, embrace your calling to make disciples, and read this book!

Dr. Susan Freese | Author of the award-winning book, *Your True Story: The 50-Day Essential Guide to Your New Life with Jesus*; founder of All In Ministries International

A generation of Christians have lost their passion to share the good news of Jesus Christ with their neighbors and the nations. *Always Going* provides a clear road map to understanding the eight simple but critical steps for every follower of Christ to gain the confidence to share the greatest truth for all mankind everywhere they go. After 20 years as a youth pastor, this book is one of the best I've ever read to help students and adults walk through the process of igniting a daily rhythm of sharing the gospel "as they go." Thank you, Andrew, for answering the Lord's call to be a voice in this generation to remind us of the urgent mission we, as believers in Jesus, have been commanded to live out. I wholeheartedly recommend this book to every church, youth group, pastor, and fellow Christian I know. We don't have time to waste, let's always go!

Dan Elkins | Executive Pastor of Next Gen-Students at Northland Church, Orlando, FL

I highly recommend Andrew Steier's insightful book on sharing the gospel. This transformative guide delves deep into understanding evangelism at a profound level, encouraging readers to embrace an outward-focused life. Steier masterfully explores the essential elements of being rooted in the gospel, experiencing heart transformation, and confidently recognizing how God uses us. He emphasizes the importance of celebrating every gospel conversation, making this book a vital resource for anyone committed to sharing their faith.

Bob Bumgarner | Lead Missional Strategist of First Coast Churches, Jacksonville, FL

Steier weaves clear teaching and engaging stories together to remind us that our love for God and others overflows from us so that we share the gift of God's love with the lost. Evangelism stems from what is inside of us—love, truth, and grace—all things the lost need from us. *Always Going* is a great reminder that evangelism comes from our love and relationship with the Father.

Stefanie Nicholson | Founder of Here2There Ministries

Too often, Christians approach Jesus' Great Commission with the same demeanor as passengers during an airplane's oxygen mask demonstration: half-listening, somewhat apprehensive, and secretly hoping they won't have to act on it. In *Always Going*, Steier focuses on the fact that we can serve others effectively only after ensuring our own spiritual well-being. This book is like a much-needed instruction guide to changing lives, starting with your own. It will captivate your attention and ignite a passion for sharing the gospel!

Paul Nather | 19-year pastor at Century Baptist Church, Bismarck, ND; Steier's former youth pastor

I found myself growing more excited with every chapter of this brilliantly crafted book on evangelism. *Always Going* is much more than a title—it is a significantly meaningful mission. Andrew seamlessly weaves the intricate fabric of doctrine, theology, and practical application into a thoroughly engaging and thoughtfully compelling must-read. This book belongs on the shelf of every believer.

Phillip Van Lear | Men's ministry leader; trained *Always Going* GO Leader; author; motivational speaker; actor

Having known Andrew for years and watching him grow from a local church youth pastor to a man on a multi-church mission, I have observed two things. Andrew is an authentic and bold visionary in his love for God's people and those not yet God's people. I was not surprised to see that authenticity and vision on every page. In fact, this book is as much an autobiography of Andrew as it is a call to the church to be *Always Going*.

Wes Slough | 35-year pastor; founder of Slough Ministries International; 25-year trainer of pastors and church-planters around the world

I've seen thousands of graduates go on to live lives of adventure, intentionality, or passion. I have rarely seen a student combine all three. Andrew Steier has the "it" factor of adventure, intentionality, and passion. I named my son after Andrew in the Bible, who was definitely an evangelist and brought people to Jesus. I am not surprised that Andrew Steier has the same first name! He has a plan and purpose to mobilize people to share their faith—always on mission, always going, always sharing the good news of Jesus. I encourage you to pick up *Always Going* and take it to heart. It could change not only your life but the lives of others for eternity.

Dr. David Olshine | Director of Youth Ministry, Family, and Culture at Columbia International University; author of *The Mystery of Silence*

No matter how deep you venture into *Always Going*, marking up every page or simply glancing through the eight elements, you will gain a more biblical understanding of how God intends for His people to reach the lost. I am both called and inspired to reflect on what God has done for me and how His love overflows from me as I reach others—not viewing people as projects but living a life of loving outreach. Knowing that I can celebrate every gospel conversation is immensely comforting, and I feel ready to expand the Kingdom of God.

Ethan Binns | High school senior; trained *Always Going* GO Leader

ALWAYSGOING

In loving memory of
Peter Kuchar

−M

ALWAYSGOING

THE JOYFUL OVERFLOW OF EVERYDAY EVANGELISM

ANDREW STEIER

Always Going
The Joyful Overflow of Everyday Evangelism

Andrew Steier

Copyright © 2024 Andrew Steier

979-8-9908720-0-4   Hardcover
979-8-9908720-1-1   Paperback
979-8-9908720-2-8   Digital

Scripture quotations taken from The Holy Bible, New International Version® NIV® Copyright © 1973, 1978, 1984, 2011 by Biblica, Inc. Used with permission. All rights reserved worldwide.

Scripture quotations marked ESV are from the ESV® (The English Standard Version®), copyright © 2001 by Crossway, a publishing ministry of Good News Publishers. Used by permission. All rights reserved.

No part of this publication may be reproduced, or stored in a retrieval system, or transmitted, in any form or by any means, mechanical, electronic, photocopying, recording or otherwise, without the prior permission of Always Going.

Typeset by www.greatwriting.org

Printed in the United States of America

Published by Always Going

Cover design by Bill Giarratana

Every purchase goes toward challenging, equipping, and sending believers to live with an outward focus.

For bulk orders, custom editions, or to request the author to speak at your event, please contact andrew@alwaysgoing.org.

Published in cooperation with Goodwill Media Services, www.goodwillmediaservices.com

To Autumn

You are my constant friend and faithful partner. Your devotion to Christ and unconditional love for others is a beautiful illustration of every word in this book.

"He must become greater; I must become less."
John 3:30

For additional resources, visit
alwaysgoing.org

CONTENTS

Foreword 13
Introduction 17
The Gospel 23
The Heart 39
The Life 55
The Lost 71
The Gap 87
The Role 109
The Plan 123
The Win 135
Always Going 149

FOREWORD

When I first met Andrew, he was a self-confessed recovering "professional Christian." That is to say, his life had consisted of being a pastor's kid, Bible college student, and most recently a full-time church staff pastor. Anyone who has experienced even one of these positions knows the internal and external pressures to be, do, and say all the right things all the time. I understand this pressure from firsthand experience, too. I knew exactly where he was and the beautiful, joy-filled life that God offers to exchange it with. Andrew was bursting with vision for God's missional call for the church to be witnesses in all the world. Yet, I sensed he was simultaneously discovering for the first time what it meant to walk with God in the yoke that Jesus promised was easy (*Matt. 11:28-30*)—a way of being with God that isn't obligatory or motivated by anything other than God's gracious love offered to us. From that time to today, Andrew has joyfully, relentlessly, and prayerfully focused his devotion on studying, teaching, and living out God's command to go make disciples. I see a modern-day Ezra in Andrew. Ezra was a priest and scribe who experienced exile with the people of Israel and faithfully *"set his heart to study the Law of the* LORD, *and to do it and to teach his statutes and rules in Israel"* (Ezra 7:10 ESV). Ezra called people back to joyful worship and stirred up revival through his teachings. I believe this book can do the same for you in your spiritual life. Andrew's history, recovery, and discovery have all converged with his calling to give us *Always Going*.

A few months ago, I invited Andrew to audit, alongside myself and another leader from our church staff, a 700-level graduate residency course on Evangelism & Discipleship. Imagine about twenty hours of lectures in five days taught by one of the foremost voices in the world on missiology, the study of Christian mission. Dr. Scott Sunquist, the president of Gordon-Conwell Theological Seminary (my alma mater), was the teaching professor. He is humble, brilliant, and deeply passionate about evangelism and global missions. He is, no doubt, an expert in the field.

The week was amazing. It was filled with learning, dreaming, and laughter at inside jokes as we passionately dug into God's call for our own lives and the global church—to joyfully join God in His redemptive mission through loving relationship. As we participated in the course together, I could see the great excitement and confidence building in Andrew's eyes. Every night of the course affirmed the work and ministry thrust of *Always Going*. I share that story for you to have confidence that the content within this

FOREWORD

book is theologically sound. Andrew skillfully explores the practical and profound connections between our Christian theology, spiritual formation, and the practice of our faith. Moreover, he communicates in a way that we can all understand. He asks probing questions in every chapter that cause us to confront our spiritual complacency, wrestle with our theological convictions, and unearth our unconscious, innermost longings to joyfully participate with God in His mission.

It's no secret that our world is insanely individualistic and selfish. The "selfie culture" pervades every square inch of our society, not just social media. However, I believe there is a generation being raised up right now who are passionately seeking a different way—the way of Jesus—a way of greatness that is humble and focuses on serving others (*Phil. 2:3-4; Matt. 20:26*). This is where true purpose, joy, and ultimate reward are found, after all. The eight elements in *Always Going* provide a tangible pathway toward developing an intentionally outward-focused life—a life needed and truly wanted by every Christian. The implementation of this content would save thousands of churches from shriveling up and dying in the years to come. Any church that grabs ahold of this could radically shift the tides not only of individual spiritual vitality, but of the growth of God's kingdom.

I've had the joy to watch Andrew come alongside new and seasoned believers, helping them discover their "gospel gaps," face their fears, and learn to boldly and joyfully join God's mission. The approach within this book is relatable and free from the shame-filled tactics of evangelism you may have experienced in the past. *Always Going* will stir your affections for Jesus, call you to a deeper prayer life with God, and completely reinvent the way you think about and talk about Christ with nonbelievers. On top of all that, you'll walk away from reading this book with a burden for the lost that is somehow still light because you will have understood your role in witness and God's role in salvation.

If you're not sure how to share Jesus with non-believing loved ones, friends, neighbors, or coworkers. . .

If you get the shivers when someone says the word evangelism. . .

If you're stuck at the loading dock with the good news and fear is holding you back. . .

Or if you've simply run out of joy and passion in sharing your faith. . .

. . .then *Always Going* is going to be a life-changing book for you. The heart of *Always Going* is that striving and performance-based Christianity would be a thing of the past and a natural overflow to witness would become normative for every believer.

I pray this book sets you free to enjoy God thoroughly and eagerly share His gift.

KYLE NELSON
Lead Pastor, Fathom Church (Jacksonville, FL)
President, Fathom Family Foundation

INTRODUCTION

OF FAITH AND FOOTBALL

I love watching football—American football, to be clear, not the more appropriately named game that actually uses *feet* to advance the ball. I'm in awe of how a seemingly normal human can throw an oblong ball sixty yards to a teammate running Olympianly fast, chased by a third guy determined to stop it all from happening. I'm mesmerized when I see it all come together.

It's easy to picture this scene, after seeing it so many times, and think, "This—this is football; superhumans performing impossible tasks, cheered on by 60,000 wild fans."

We see the moment—the product. What we *don't* see is the father who tossed a ball to his son for the very first time twenty years ago. We don't see the years of training, all the times these athletes chose a salad over a burger, or the late nights studying film. We don't see the coaches, the weight room, or the thousands of times that same play went wrong in practice. Our eyes are fixed on the *product*, not the journey.

It's not hard to see evangelism in the very same way. Just like the word *football* conjures images of screaming fans and touchdown dances, the word *evangelism* makes us picture a specific moment or event—a product. No wonder we get nervous whenever someone mentions sharing the gospel. It's one thing to *know* the basics and a simple method or two, but a completely different thing to regularly *share* what we believe with the people we love in a way that isn't awkward, judgmental, or forced—not to mention how scary it can be! We feel unqualified, ill-equipped, or unworthy, much like I would feel if asked to throw the final pass in the Superbowl.

I've watched these thoughts decimate the motivation and confidence of too many Bible-believing, church-attending, Christ-loving people. One thing is clear: There is a problem with the way many Christians view evangelism—a negative stigma that sends a shiver down our spines and keeps our lips sealed.

But what if we've gotten it wrong? What if I told you

that evangelism is not what we've made it out to be—that the paralyzing fear of awkward conversations or blatant rejection is completely understandable because we've misunderstood something about God's mission to reach the lost?

What if all those who have actively avoided or given up on sharing their faith considered simply putting their helmets back on and showing up for practice? No Superbowl, no audience, just a Cobb salad and some jumping jacks. Well, if that was the case, I think we'd have a few more evangelists on our hands, don't you?

Take you, for instance. By even reading this, you are deciding to take your next step of faith—equipping yourself to join God's mission. You are looking outside the walls of your own personal faith toward others who need to hear the life-changing message of Jesus. You're also responding to the Great Commandment *(Matt. 22:36-40)* and the Great Commission *(Matt. 28:18-20)*—to love the Lord your God with everything you have, to love your neighbor as yourself, and to go make disciples. You're either getting into the game for the very first time or getting back in the game after a few quarters on the bench.

What follows isn't just another method or trick to add to your evangelistic arsenal. It's an outward-focused *worldview* that will have you looking for gospel conversations with anyone, at any time, and anywhere—a fresh lens to help you see yourself and others as God intended.

Without a proper outward-focused worldview, evangelism becomes a task, a product, or a destination. What was intended as an everyday overflow mutates into an obligatory event—a job rather than a joy.

Instead of focusing on the finish line, let's take some time to understand evangelism on a deeper level, looking at what comes *before* each gospel conversation. Let's develop confidence and boldness in our witness while simultaneously growing closer to God.

On this journey, you will encounter what I like to call the *elements of an outward-focused life*:

> The Gospel—Am I rooted in the gospel?
> The Heart—Has my heart been transformed?
> The Life—Does my life reflect what I claim to believe?
> The Lost—Am I motivated to reach others?
> The Gap—Am I hesitant to share the gospel?
> The Role—Am I confident in how God uses me?
> The Plan—Is my preparation fueled by love?
> The Win—Am I celebrating every gospel conversation?

These eight elements work together to strengthen our dependence upon God *and* propel us toward those who don't know Him. They are the salad, the bench press, and the long hours of practice that help us grow at the right pace, even if it isn't the easiest or quickest. When we see evangelism rightly—as an overflow—and when we take time to develop an outward-focused worldview, we'll find ourselves seeking out gospel conversations because it's *who we are*, not just what we do.

Thank you from the bottom of my heart for being bold enough to take your next step of faith. Thank you for beginning the journey that will lead you toward a dark world with the light of the gospel. Now grab your helmet because practice just started.

Andrew Steier
Founder
Always Going

ASK YOURSELF

- What images and emotions come to mind when I hear the word *evangelism*?
- On a scale of one to ten, how comfortable do I feel sharing my faith?
- How often do I think about the faith of others?
- Have I taken myself out of the game?

Element One
THE GOSPEL

Am I rooted in the gospel?

MISSIONAL MOTORS

Our first stop on the road to an outward-focused life is one that many people pass by. Like the gas station three miles out of town, we don't feel the immediate need to fill the tank so we hurry on our way, destination in mind.

I have spent my fair share of time gripping the steering wheel with white knuckles, praying that the Lord would grant me unlimited unleaded because of my absentmindedness, pride, or poor planning. Gasoline seems like a silly thing to forget on a road trip, but I bet you've experienced something similar. Whether it's speeding past a gas station, skipping breakfast before a workout, or staying up all night before an exam, it's easy to discount how crucial *fuel* is in our daily lives. Our fixation on the destination, product, or event distracts us from one of the most foundational pieces of a life on mission.

And so, as we slow down and consider the journey, let's begin by asking: If gasoline fuels our cars and protein fuels our workouts, what fuels evangelism? What keeps our missional motors running? What is the thing that both turns and keeps our focus *outward*, toward those who need Christ? You guessed it: *The Gospel*.

BEST NEWS EVER

The gospel is not a quartet of books in the Bible, it's not a genre of choir music, and it's certainly not a collection of self-help affirmations. The gospel is, quite simply put, the best news we could possibly imagine. In fact, the word *gospel* literally means *good news*. But what is this news?

Author J. Mack Stiles says, "The gospel is the joyful message from God that leads us to salvation."[1] It's news that reminds us of our identity and purpose, helps us make sense of the world around us, and gives us hope for the future.

The gospel both *is* and *isn't* every word in the Bible. Many would argue that the whole Bible communicates the gospel message, and I would agree. Every God-breathed verse is an important thread in the tapestry of God's redemptive

---

[1] J. Mack Stiles, *Evangelism: How the Whole Church Speaks of Jesus* (Wheaton, IL: Crossway, 2014), 33

story. Others would argue that the name of Noah's oldest son isn't necessary for salvation, and I would, again, agree. The amazing thing about the gospel is its ability to communicate a lifetime of learning in a few simple words. Let me use an example.

THE SIMPLICITY OF STAR WARS

When I was seven years old, my parents showed me *Star Wars: Episode IV—A New Hope*. I remember it vividly because I had never seen anything like it before. I watched in awe as lasers flashed on the screen, lightsabers clashed, and music swelled during dramatic moments. It was a far cry from *Sesame Street*. My life changed that day. I was introduced to something so awesome and so gripping that my very identity was never the same.

I became a devoted *Star Wars* fan. My desires were changed as I longed for *Star Wars* action figures and toy blasters. My thoughts were changed, leading me to daydream about what it would be like to wield a lightsaber of my own. And that was only the beginning! Did you know that there are *more Star Wars movies*?

Here's my point. My love of *Star Wars* led to a lifetime of learning. I watch the movies and TV shows, play the games, and read the books. I even have a *Star Wars Encyclopedia* full of obscure facts and diagrams. But if you asked seven-year-old Andrew to explain *Star Wars*, I could sum it up with three words. Good overcomes evil. These three words *both* accurately represent the entirety of *Star Wars and* barely scratch the surface of what it has to offer.

We can view the gospel message in the same way. The eight words we will use to remember it *both* accurately represent Christianity *and* barely scratch the surface of what a life with Christ has to offer.

EIGHT SIMPLE WORDS

At its core, the gospel message consists of four parts that work in perfect harmony:

- Holy God
- Sinful Man
- Perfect Savior
- Eternal Destiny

Each part represents hours, months, and years of deeper understanding. Don't believe me? Well, why don't you give me a call when you've completely mastered the holiness of God? See what I mean? It takes *years*.

I was drawn into a love of *Star Wars* in its simplicity, then grew in my knowledge of it through years of deeper study. We must be careful not to require from others in a moment what took us years to understand. In fact, some of us may not understand the basics of the gospel as much as we think. Let me explain.

In 2022, I led a one-day evangelism workshop for about sixty believers in Jacksonville, Florida. Eight different churches were represented in the audience, but despite differences in church size, denomination, age, gender, and spiritual maturity, a pre-workshop survey revealed that only twenty-five percent of those in attendance felt very confident that they could communicate the basics of the gospel message. Now, I'm not sharing that to criticize or shame anyone, only to highlight the importance of the gospel in evangelism. Keep in mind that those surveyed were Christ-followers who committed eight straight hours to an event centered on evangelism. Imagine the response of the average churchgoer! If we truly desire to live outward-focused lives, we must become comfortable, confident, and fluent in the basics of the gospel message.

HOLY GOD

Like all things, the gospel begins with God. God has always existed as Father, Son, and Spirit. He is perfect and holy in every way. God didn't need anything, but, out of His great love, He created us to rule and enjoy life with Him in the Garden of Eden, paradise on earth. We are the pinnacle of His creation, made in His very image *(Gen. 1:26-27)*.

We could go on, diving deeper into God's attributes like mercy, love, patience, grace, righteousness, wrath, justice, and more. We could search through Scripture to find descriptors of God like Wonderful Counselor, Mighty God, Everlasting Father, or Prince of Peace *(Isa. 9:6)*. The depth of this part of the gospel is limitless, and yet we only need to wade ankle-deep into God's holiness as we introduce the gospel to those who need it.

SINFUL MAN

The good news starts with a good God, but it doesn't end there. Despite being given all things, including an intimate relationship with God, we weren't satisfied. We wanted more, were deceived into disobeying Him, and brought another *way* into creation that contradicted God's perfect way *(Gen. 3)*. We call this way sin, and it stands as a barrier between us and a holy God.

We see sin all around us. There are certain actions universally condemned by humanity, even those who don't believe in any sort of higher power. Understanding how our sin plays a role in God's mission to restore mankind is key to having real, genuine conversations with people struggling to make sense of a broken world.

PERFECT SAVIOR

The gospel doesn't end with our separation from God. It wouldn't be very good news if it did. God didn't eliminate us, opting to start over. He moved forward with redemption on His mind. God sent His Son, Jesus, to take our place. The payment for sin is death, and Jesus, the only sinless one, willingly gave His life to make a way for us to be adopted into God's family forever before defeating death by being resurrected from the grave.

Our minds have a hard time fathoming a love like that. Many people find it completely unbelievable, not feeling worthy of such a sacrifice or scoffing at the idea of God lowering Himself to such a humiliating display. I'll be honest; even in my complete surrender to Christ, I struggle to grasp why a God so holy would die for a sinner like me.

ETERNAL DESTINY

Our last point is one of great hope but also great warning. When we turn from our sin of unbelief and trust wholly in God for salvation, we're adopted into His eternal family and given a new heart that longs for His way. When we fall short of His standard of holiness, we look to Jesus who paid our debt and freely forgives. We grow more like Christ each day until we go to be with Him forever in heaven. Conversely, those who refuse to repent and surrender their own way are eternally separated from God in hell.

This is the great question looming in the back of every person's mind. "What happens after my time on earth is done?" The gospel gives great clarity and invites those who surrender into the family of God.

GOSPEL HARMONY

These four parts, expressed in eight simple words, are the core. They are the foundation we build upon as we share the hope of Jesus with others. But that's not all! Each part plays a distinct and critical role in the overall message. Ask yourself: "If any one part was left out, would the gospel stop being good news?" Let's follow that rabbit trail for just a moment.

What would happen if we left *Holy God* out of the gospel? Well, we'd also have to throw out things like our creation, our purpose and meaning, and our innate sense of right and wrong. Our basis for all order and morality would collapse, not to mention the hopelessness of being left alone to figure out life for ourselves without a guiding light. But the thing that would sting the most if we left out God, I believe, is love. God created humanity out of a desire to love. He sustains us with His love, we can rest in His love, and we can trust that His love is good *because* He is holy.

What if we left out *Sinful Man*? Surely that would be okay to omit, right? Not if we want to explain the absolute chaos of this broken world around us. The fact that man sinned and that sin separates us from a holy God is oddly comforting. Think of it this way. If nothing ever went wrong, it would mean that God created the world as it is today—broken. But God didn't create a broken world. He created a perfect paradise and asked us to trust Him. Our sin separates us from God, but it's a key part of the good news that we *must* include.

Okay, so both of those are important, but what would happen if we left out our *Perfect Savior*? I probably don't have to go very deep here. This would be like leaving Neo out of *The Matrix*, Luke out of *Star Wars*, or Frodo out of *Lord of the Rings*. All hope is lost without the hero!

Finally, would the gospel still be good news if we left out our *Eternal Destiny*? We're back to where we started—the questions looming in everyone's mind. "What happens next?" "Why should we believe the gospel?" Leaving out *Eternal Destiny* robs us of the story's ending. God was with man in the beginning *(Gen. 1:26-30)* and desires to be with man in the end *(Rev. 21:3)*.

Despite its simplicity, the gospel must be shared in its entirety. My pastor often says, "Brevity with completeness is a virtue." He says it jokingly when I begin to ramble, but there is real truth in his words. Brevity is important, but it's only useful coupled with completeness. Many people have abandoned certain parts of the gospel to make it more appealing or palatable, but in doing so they've robbed it of its beauty and power.

GOSPEL FLUENCY

It's not only important that we *know* the gospel, but that we can *communicate* it naturally. Raise your hand if you've ever been part of an awkward presentation where it was clear the speaker *knew* the information but didn't really *know* the information—fluency.

Think back to the survey I handed out in Florida. The question wasn't, "Do you know and believe the basics of the gospel message?" It was, "If asked, could you *communicate* the basics of the gospel message?" I already mentioned that every attendee professed faith in Christ, so, in other words, they've staked their entire eternity on something that seventy-five percent of them couldn't put into words.

Fluency isn't information; it's practice. It overflows *from* us; it's not merely coaxed out of us. When I think of this concept, I'm reminded of the trip I took to Africa as a teenage boy. I accompanied my youth group to the country of Cameroon, a place I had never been. I didn't bother learning the language or anything about the culture, so when I got there, all I could do was nod, gesture, and attempt to use 2008's version of a translation app. I wasn't fluent. Even if I *did* study for hours and learn all the information I could, I wouldn't be fluent. I would stumble my way through the language because it wouldn't come naturally.

In the time I've spent working in and with local churches, I've had hundreds of conversations about the gospel. Don't check my math, but it seems like nine out of every ten times someone is asked, "What is the gospel?" the answer is, "Jesus died on the cross for your sins." This is where the tension between information and fluency becomes so important. I'll use an example.

> CHRISTIAN: You should believe the gospel.
> NON-CHRISTIAN: What's the gospel?
> CHRISTIAN: It's the good news that Jesus died on the cross for your sins!
> NON-CHRISTIAN: Why? I never asked Him to do that. I'm actually okay.

Let's pause for a moment. Where would you go from here? This is a scenario I've experienced many times, both myself and as I talk with believers about their evangelistic encounters. It highlights two major needs: the *harmony* of the gospel message and our *fluency* in it. If we run into evangelism armed with only information, our conversations become presentations. We're only able to share what we've carefully prepared and memorized. However, being fluent in the gospel means I can flow naturally in whatever direction the conversation turns.

> NON-CHRISTIAN: Why? I never asked Him to do that. I'm actually okay.
> FLUENT-CHRISTIAN: I completely understand. But have you noticed how messed up the world around us is?
> NC: Yeah, I guess so.

FC: Well, I believe that God didn't create things like this, but humans actually disobeyed God, leading to a broken world.

NC: So, what does that have to do with me?

FC: It means that we're all sinners, we all mess up, and we're all in need of a Savior to fix our relationship with God.

NC: Makes sense, I guess.

FC: So, when I say Jesus died for your sins, I mean that He made a way for you to be right with God and wipe away everything you've ever done wrong. All He asks is that you trust Him.

NC: What do you mean, "trust Him"?

FC: I mean surrender your life to Him and live His way. We read about it in the Bible. I can get you one and we can read it together if you want. But it also means we get to be with God one day in heaven, not based on how good we are, but our surrender to Jesus.

A deep understanding of the gospel's harmony paired with a willingness, fluency, and confidence to go wherever the conversation leads are key to living an outward-focused life.

PRACTICE MAKES ~~PERFECT~~ IT EASIER

So, how can we become more gospel fluent? How can we keep from becoming rigid and stuck in presentations instead of having loving and natural conversations? Practice.

You've heard the old adage, "Practice makes perfect," but let's not shoot for perfection quite yet. How about this? Practice makes it *easier*. The only way to become more comfortable and confident with the gospel message is to practice! This is the first of many times I'll mention practice.

When learning a second language, is it wise to speak that language only around native speakers? No! That's ridiculous. We practice at home, in the car, in the shower, to our pets, and in a hundred other places, so when we finally need to use the bathroom at the Eiffel Tower, we can discreetly whisper, *"Où sont les toilettes?"* to the nearest security guard instead of doing the potty dance and making wild flushing gestures.

The first thing you can practice with a friend, spouse, parent, or pastor is your understanding of gospel harmony. Have someone you trust ask you about each part of the gospel: *Holy God, Sinful Man, Perfect Savior,* and *Eternal Destiny.* Share what you know about each idea and why it's important to the overall message. And when you're finished with that, make some observations, and start again!

Another great way to practice is to flex your fluency. Begin sharing the gospel by starting with *Eternal Destiny* and navigating to the three other parts. Then begin with *Sinful Man* and do it again. Seamlessly including every part of the gospel while having a natural conversation is the goal. Have your partner test you by asking hard questions and playing devil's advocate. Remember, you are loved, you are safe, and discomfort in growth is normal.

Then, and this is the fun part, switch places. Observe and take some notes on how your partner shares the gospel. Practice may not make perfect, but believe me, it sure makes it easier.

SAME MESSAGE, DIFFERENT METHODS

If you grew up in church, you probably encountered one of about a thousand gospel-sharing methods. The Romans Road walks believers through the gospel by highlighting four verses: Romans 3:23, 6:23, 5:8, then 10:9.

Stiles, who gave us our definition of *gospel*, likes to ask four often-asked questions:

- Who is God?
- Why are we in such a mess?
- What did Christ do?
- How can we get back to God?[2]

Other methods include easily distributable tracts, the Three Circles, the Bridge, the Four Spiritual Laws, the EvangeCube, and even the "gospel fuzzies" my kids brought home from Sunday school on a bracelet one day. There are hundreds, if not thousands, of ways to communicate the basics of the gospel.

Now pay close attention, because this is the most important thing I'll say in this entire chapter. It doesn't matter which of these methods you choose as long as you communicate the gospel clearly and completely. One denomination might prefer one way, and another might prefer something different. People are constantly innovating new ways to share the gospel, but let's be crystal clear. *Methods* may change, but the *message* never has and never will.

The essence of living an outward-focused life is not memorization and regurgitation, but loving discernment

---

[2] J. Mack Stiles, *Evangelism: How the Whole Church Speaks of Jesus* (Wheaton, IL: Crossway, 2014), 33

and intentional preparation. So, memorize a method, or two, or thirty. It doesn't matter if it's a cube, an intriguing question or two, or some fuzzies. The question we should all be asking ourselves is this: "Why *this* method with *this* person?" As we'll discuss in later chapters, everyone has a point of greatest gospel need. It's our job to wisely discern *how* we share the same message with different people from all walks of life.

ROOTED

The gospel is only the first element of an outward-focused life, but I'm sure you can see how crucial it is. It is the fuel in our tanks as we drive toward the lost.

Each one of these elements begins with a question, the question for this chapter being, "Am I *rooted* in the gospel?" Not, "Do I know the gospel?" or "Am I fluent in the gospel?" Those are important questions, but they pale in comparison to the first.

Evangelism is not an event. It's an overflow. Like studying for a test just to forget all the information the following day, it's easy to gorge on the gospel, share it, then walk away feeling satisfied. But that isn't the life we're called to live as followers of Christ. I love David's words in Psalm 63.

> *You, God, are my God, earnestly I seek you; I thirst for you, my whole being longs for you, in a dry and parched land where there is no water. (v. 1)*

We are called to reflect on the gospel daily, to fill up at the well of God's goodness and grace, to remember what's been done for us, to surrender the hidden parts of our lives, and to overflow into others. Being rooted in the gospel means we are receiving constant nourishment from God, not taking a trip to the spiritual buffet once a week.

And so, as this element comes to a close and we move on to the next, I invite you to examine your own understanding of and fluency in the good news and ask yourself, "Am I rooted in the gospel?"

ASK YOURSELF

- How confident do I feel communicating the basics of the gospel?
- What are some of the best ways I've heard the gospel presented? What are some strengths and weaknesses of each way?
- Why does discernment matter when deciding how to share the gospel?
- Why is it important to be rooted in the gospel before sharing it?

Element Two
THE HEART

Has my heart been transformed?

SECONDHAND JOY

Life-changing moments are contagious. I can vividly recall the day my best friend got his first vehicle—a black Ford Ranger. I'm not sure which one of us was more excited when he called to tell me the news. I remember pacing in anticipation as I waited for him to pick me up for the first time, the pure joy of cruising around town together, and the freedom of finally having some wheels for ourselves.

It's not hard to figure out why *he* would be excited, is it? He got to sit behind the wheel of this brand-new gift, feeling the A/C blow on his face and changing the radio station at will, but why would *I*, sitting at home, be so excited by someone else's experience? It's simple, really. It's because he told me all about it. He described it to me in a way that made it sound irresistible. I heard the joy in his voice as he explained how this simple gift had and would forever change his life.

GOD'S GOOD GIFT

You can probably already see where I'm headed with this analogy. As Christians, we've been given an incredible gift—something far more exciting than a midsize truck with low mileage and only a few scratches and dents. If our first element is to be believed, we have uninhibited access to the God of creation through faith and surrender. We have a personal relationship with the Alpha and Omega—the Beginning and the End. We've been given a gift that has and will forever change our lives.

Scripture describes it this way.

> *I will give you a new heart and put a new spirit in you; I will remove from you your heart of stone and give you a heart of flesh. And I will put my Spirit in you and move you to follow my decrees and be careful to keep my laws.* (Ezek. 36:26-27)

What are we given as made-new children of God? We're given a new heart. No, not a physical heart that pumps blood to our extremities, but a new *identity* that changes us at our deepest, most intimate level. The gospel claims that we are separated from God, unable to bridge the gap of His holiness on our own due to faulty equipment—a cold, dead heart of stone. But God promises to give us a new, living heart of flesh, a heart that longs for His way above our own. It's a heart that is no longer enslaved to sinful desires but led by the Spirit of God.

The apostle Paul used the example of adoption to describe what happens when we surrender to God, calling us children of God and co-heirs with Christ.

> *For those who are led by the Spirit of God are the children of God. The Spirit you received does not make you slaves, so that you live in fear again; rather, the Spirit you received brought about your adoption to sonship. And by him we cry, "Abba, Father." The Spirit himself testifies with our spirit that we are God's children. Now if we are children, then we are heirs—heirs of God and co-heirs with Christ, if indeed we share in his sufferings in order that we may also share in his glory. (Rom. 8:14-17)*

MORE THAN A MESSAGE

I could go on for pages, chapters, and dozens of books without fully capturing the gift of salvation and what it means for believers, but let's take a step back and ask an important question. Why are we spending so much time talking about *us* in a book about reaching *them*? Well, if our first element, *The Gospel,* helped us lay a foundation for healthy, outward-focused evangelism, our second element, *The Heart,* begins construction.

Think back to my friend and his truck. *He* was given a gift. *He* experienced the fullness of that gift. *He* felt the weight and responsibility of caring for and nurturing that gift. So where did *my* excitement come from? It came from the phone call. I wasn't a part of the purchasing process. I didn't pick out the color. I wasn't handed the keys. And yet, when he called to tell me about the gift given to *him*—not to me—I was elated, both for my friend whom I love, and the prospect that I could experience even a fraction of his joy for myself. Let's put it all together.

The gospel is simply a promise—the promise of a new heart for those who turn to God. That message, by itself, cannot save. It is an invitation to surrender, not a magic formula that we chant in the direction of nonbelievers. We are called to share this message with others, but what begins as simple, albeit exciting, information becomes something entirely different when we have experienced its transformative power for ourselves.

Sure, my friend could have called me to talk about the car-buying process. We could have looked through a magazine and circled all the cars and trucks that we wanted someday, but the information came to life when he called to tell me it had happened to *him*. We've been given the most contagious gift imaginable—a new heart drenched in the Spirit of God. And I believe that this new heart is one of the most effective tools given to us by God to reach the lost.

THE HEART

SOMEBODY TESTIFY

Let me tell you a little bit about teenage Andrew. No, I didn't do hard drugs or even soft drugs, for that matter. I didn't steal cars or get into fistfights, but it wouldn't take much time for you to see how far I was from the Lord. Manipulation was the name of my game. I was arrogant, rude, offensive, and downright cruel sometimes. I sought validation by tearing others down or finding some insecurity of theirs to expose. I could go on, but I'd rather not. You get the idea, right?

Here's the point. If I called up Sam, Ashley, Tyler, or Derek, they would confirm what I just told you. They could give you instances, recalling specific and detailed memories of my teenage blunders—proof. On the flipside, you could come to the church I attend now and talk to Charlie, Justin, Allyson, or Rachel, and they would all tell you a different story. They would hopefully tell you that I'm not rude, manipulative, or cruel anymore, and that I find my joy in building others up rather than tearing them down. Something changed. Something objectively and verifiably caused me to transform.

The word *testimony* gets thrown around a lot in Christian circles, and for many people it is simply a nice story about how they became a Christian. But it is *so* much more! *Testimony* is just the noun form of the word *testify*. When I think of testifying, my mind is immediately drawn to one of my favorite TV genres, courtroom dramas. In these shows, silver-tongued attorneys stand before solemn juries, hurling question after question at emotional witnesses on the stand. We know this scene. In fact, our entire legal system is built upon this process. It often looks something like this.

> ATTORNEY: Tell us, ma'am, what you saw the night of the crash.
> WITNESS 1: A man in a red car hit a woman on a yellow bike.
> ATTORNEY: And you, sir, what did *you* see that night?
> WITNESS 2: I saw a red car hit a woman on a yellow bike.
> ATTORNEY: Finally, I ask you, young lady, what did you see while you were playing with chalk in the front yard?
> WITNESS 3: The man in the car ran over the yellow bike.

What can we deduce from this simple scenario? If you were on the jury, what would your verdict be? Well, I can only assume it's the same as mine. A man driving a red car hit a woman riding a yellow bike. Signed, sealed, delivered. We send people to jail, levy enormous fines, and make life-altering decisions based on testimony. The *subjective* memories of these witnesses are seen as *objective* evidence when repeated and confirmed by multiple sources. Here's where it gets really cool.

Multiple witnesses could testify that I was one way as a teenager, and multiple witnesses could testify that I am completely different as an adult. The life-altering event in question? My belief in the power of the gospel, complete surrender to the Lord, and radical identity change. My testimony is not a nice story of how I met Jesus; rather, it is objective evidence proving both the power and reality of the gospel. It's the life application of gospel information.

"But you're just one person," you might think. "Why

should anyone believe your subjective experience?" Great question. Except I am not the only one who has experienced this phenomenon. The gospel's power and reality are confirmed by the transformation of every believer in human history. The apostle Paul was objectively and verifiably one way, met Jesus, and became a new man *(1 Tim. 1:12-17)*. Martin Luther, father of the Reformation, was objectively and verifiably one way, met Jesus in the 1500s, and became a new man. Alicia, my sister whom you probably don't know, was objectively and verifiably one way, met Jesus, and became a new woman. The evidence is overwhelming, and the verdict is clear. The message of the gospel leads to complete life transformation in those who believe.

ANATOMY OF AN ENCOUNTER

When we see our testimonies as powerful evidence rather than pleasant stories, we begin to understand how they fit into this discussion about evangelism. They are tools given to us by God to reach others—tools to be used, not set on the shelf to collect dust. So, how do we use them?

I like to divide my testimony into three distinct parts. You may have heard similar verbiage, but much like the gospel, the main points remain the same.

- Who was I before I knew God?
- What happened that caused me to follow Him?
- Who am I now that He has made me new?

Picture the witness stand from our courtroom scene. If the validity and power of the gospel were on trial, what would your evidence be—your testimony that proves the gospel to be true? I've never personally been called as a witness in a trial, but I can assure you that I wouldn't lackadaisically saunter through the story of my entire childhood. I would give the most pertinent information—the facts that proved my point.

The same should be said about our Christian testimonies. I love the story in John 9 of the man born blind. This man encountered Jesus and experienced His power by receiving his sight, only to be interrogated by the persnickety religious leaders.

> *"How then were your eyes opened?" [the Pharisees] asked. [The man born blind] replied, "The man they call Jesus made some mud and put it on my eyes. He told me to go to Siloam and wash. So I went and washed, and then I could see." (vv. 10-11)*

The Pharisees were on the hunt, trying to deduce how this miracle could have happened only to end up on a wild-goose chase without many answers. Finally, they ended up back at the man, exasperated and frustrated.

> *A second time they summoned the man who had been blind. "Give glory to God by telling the truth," they said. "We know this man is a sinner." He replied, "Whether he is a sinner or not, I don't know. One thing I do know. I was blind but now I see!" (vv. 24-25)*

I love this story because it so closely mirrors our own experience with Jesus. "I don't know all the details. I don't understand how a holy God could save someone like me, but I was one way, I met Jesus, and now I'm completely different." Sharing a story of transformation with others doesn't need to be much more complicated than that.

HEART TO HEART

Speaking of stories, here's mine. I'm a pastor's kid from an uncommonly wonderful family. Like many other church kids, I rebelled as a teenager because I thought I knew better than everyone else. I surrendered to Jesus in college after experiencing the darkness and loneliness of living life on my own and ran to Him for companionship and direction. I know my story pretty well. What I *don't* know is your story. I don't know why you turned to Jesus or even *if* you've turned to Him. I don't know how hard or easy your life has been or if you've been struggling this week.

I may not know the details, but I *am* certain that you were once (or still are) far from God, experiencing life and trying to blaze a trail on your own. I am certain that Jesus wants a deep, personal relationship with you. And I am certain that your life has or will change radically and joyfully by surrendering to Him.

I already mentioned the importance of seeing evangelism as a conversation rather than a presentation. Sure, if you get the chance to present the gospel to a group, present it well, but it's easy to treat our individual encounters like one-way streets, too. The news of my friend's new car would have felt different if I was one in a sixty-person group text. The fact that he specifically called to have an individual conversation with me about the good news communicated his love for me and his desire for me to experience a part of his joy.

In our conversations with others, it's important to not just talk, but listen. We may have life-changing things to say, but our love for others is what brings the information to life. As I said, I know my story and I don't know yours, but through intentional conversation, real interest, and genuine care, I can discover your point of greatest gospel need. I can learn your fears, your hesitations, and your doubts. I might even discover that our stories overlap! Even though I'm a pastor's kid from North Dakota and you're an army brat from everywhere, maybe we both experienced loneliness that can only be satisfied in Christ. And suddenly, not through presentation but conversation, I have a red carpet to share the gospel in a way that will be most clearly understood and warmly welcomed.

THE VINE AND THE BRANCHES

Our second element of an outward-focused life is far from over. The question "Has my heart been transformed?" is so important because it reminds us of the moment we were adopted by God, given a new heart, and declared His. However, despite the magnitude of that moment, *The Heart* plays an even larger role in evangelism than a simple reminder.

Someone once asked me, "Why doesn't God simply zap us into heaven once we begin a relationship with Him? Wouldn't that be better?" I was so certain of my answer. I responded, "Because our purpose as believers is to share the gospel, and we can't do that if we're not here on earth."

THE HEART

I wasn't wrong, but I also wasn't completely right. Perhaps my answer raises some red flags for you. Perhaps not. Let me explain.

I spent the majority of my teenage, college, and young adult years misunderstanding my relationship with God. I pictured God like an employee would think about his boss. "He hired me, and I'm eternally grateful. I get all sorts of awesome blessings from this job, but I'd better *do* the job or the boss will be mad." In this scenario, the employee is both grateful *and* beholden to the boss. He works hard, proves his worth, and gets results which end in a reward.

When we see God this way, it's easy to think, "He created me and saved me. My response is to work for Him, specifically evangelize, *so that* He will love me, bless me, and be proud of me." But here's the thing about conditional clauses: You really have to get the order right. As a young man, I didn't necessarily get the facts wrong, just the order.

When I talk about *The Heart* as an element of an outward-focused worldview, I really mean our relationship with and identity in Christ. So, what *is* the correct order? How *should* I view my relationship with God? You might want to highlight this part because it's easy to forget.

God created me and saved me because He loves me unconditionally. Nothing I do or don't do will change His affection for me. He calls me to live a certain way for my greatest good and His greatest glory. When I succeed, He is pleased, but loves me just the same. When I fail, He forgives and loves me just the same. My *work* for God is an overflow of my love for Him, not a way to earn it.

Instead of viewing God like my boss, I should see Him as I see my spouse. I do the dishes, not to earn my wife's love, but *because* I love her. Her love is the thing that motivates me to work, do, and act.

C.S. Lewis sums it up beautifully in his book, *Mere Christianity*.

> That is why the Christian is in a different position from other people who are trying to be good. They hope, by being good, to please God if there is one; or—if they think there is not—at least they hope to deserve approval from good men. But the Christian thinks any good he does comes from the Christ-life inside him. He does not think God will love us because we are good, but that God will make us good because He loves us; just as the roof of a greenhouse does not attract the sun because it is bright, but becomes bright because the sun shines on it.[3]

If you're not convinced by Lewis, Jesus Himself explains how effectiveness in God's kingdom works—the order.

> *Remain in me, as I also remain in you. No branch can bear fruit by itself; it must remain in the vine. Neither can you bear fruit unless you remain in me. I am the vine; you are the branches. If you remain in me and I in you, you will bear much fruit; apart from me you can do nothing. (John 15:4-5)*

Before I understood this concept, I worked desperately to produce results. I wanted to *save people for God*. So, I

---

[3] C.S. Lewis, *Mere Christianity* (New York: HarperCollins, 2001), 63

would work, work, work, then approach Him with my results, asking, "Are you proud of me yet? Did I work hard enough for you to love me?" As absurd as that sounds, it's an easy trap to fall into, but when we take a step back and remember the essence of the gospel, we realize that God's love doesn't work like that. Trying to earn God's love is like a dead branch lying in the grass, working as hard as it can to produce an apple so the tree will let it back on. Backwards.

Jesus tells us to abide *in Him* before we try to produce anything *for Him.* Surrendered, Spirit-led people are how God has chosen to advance His kingdom—intimacy over ability. In fact, we are *only* useful and effective in His redemptive mission when we are in lockstep with Him.

FILL MY CUP

I love using the word *overflow* when discussing evangelism. It's such a perfect image to help us keep things in order. Picture a cup from your kitchen cabinet. As you reach up to grab it, is it overflowing? Is it spilling over into other cups? Of course not. It's empty. So, what has to happen before it can overflow? It needs to be filled.

If evangelism is an overflow, my day-to-day relationship with God is how I fill my cup. My intimacy with Jesus determines my effectiveness in His kingdom, not the other way around. If my life is an empty cup but my desire is to overflow into others, it's critical that I regularly fill from the source that never runs dry.

This is why our hearts are so important in evangelism. Just like a branch is powerless to produce fruit when separated from the tree and a cup is powerless to quench thirst without first being filled, we are powerless to participate in God's mission when we are far from Christ. Remember Jesus' words, *"Apart from me, you can do nothing."*

The good news is that nothing pleases Him more than filling the cups of His children. We're invited to know Him intimately, to walk with Him daily, to seek His guidance and wisdom, and to imitate Him—not to *earn* His love, but *because* of His love.

Let's get practical. How can we tell if we're truly abiding in Christ? Here's a short exercise I came up with to help me calibrate. First, I reflect on my thoughts, impulses, desires, and reactions over the last few weeks, taking note of any trends. What do I notice? Have I been more loving or more hateful recently? More joyful or more melancholy? Have my days been protected by peace or shrouded in arguments? Have I been patient, kind, faithful, and gentle, or nitpicky, rude, two-faced, and harsh? Feel free to think of as many opposing attitudes as you can, and simply ask, "What is the condition of my heart?"

Self-reflection before sharing the gospel is important, but only useful if the results are surrendered to the Lord. Remember, there is no condemnation for those who are in Christ *(Rom. 8:1)*. Guilt and shame are not the goal. So, how can I navigate my own shortcomings without feeling unqualified or unworthy? By turning to the one who changed my heart.

Oh, I was really rude this week? "Lord, forgive me and help me to remember your kindness so I can be kind." Was

I harsh with my children? "God, I need your help to slow down and be more gentle. You are so gentle with me, and I'm grateful. Help me."

Caring for our hearts, filling our cups, or abiding in the Vine—use whichever example makes sense to you. This practice plays such an enormous role in our motivation and ability to effectively share the good news.

HEART CHECK

The Gospel and *The Heart*. Am I rooted in the gospel? Do I know it? Can I communicate it? Has my heart been transformed *by* it? Has God redeemed my story and given me the gift of His Spirit? Can I rest in His love for me and begin to overflow into others as I regularly turn to Him for nourishment?

Evangelism begins in the mind and in the heart, not the mouth—what we believe, not just the words we say. When the truth of the gospel catches fire in the hearts of those who believe it, true evangelism is right around the corner.

ASK YOURSELF

- Have I ever experienced something so great that I couldn't help but tell others?
- Why is a believer's testimony so important? Why is *my* testimony important?
- Have I ever felt like my spiritual cup is empty? What are some practical ways I can fill my cup and keep it full?

Element Three
THE LIFE

*Does my life reflect what
I claim to believe?*

UNCONVINCING AMBASSADORS

There are few things more amusing to me than celebrities in TV commercials. From twelve-time NBA All-Star, Shaquille O'Neal, explaining why I need cut-rate car insurance to Grammy-winner and all-around bad boy, Ozzy Osbourne, suggesting I purchase my next TV at Best Buy; I love seeing out-of-place spokespeople.

On their own, car insurance and electronics aren't very funny or absurd. Shaq and Ozzy aren't either. What I find so interesting is the *juxtaposition* of product and spokesperson. In my mind, a millionaire NBA All-Star has no business suggesting affordable car insurance, and a fight-the-power rockstar probably isn't the most reliable authority on nationwide electronics superstores. Something just feels. . . off.

I think, "There is no way Shaq's thirty-seven cars are insured by *that* company, and Ozzy probably has no idea where his TV came from." When you strip away the humor and star power, it becomes clear that these men are extremely unconvincing ambassadors for their respective products—so much so, that I chuckle every time I see them on screen.

Whether we realize it or not, we signed up to be ambassadors the moment we surrendered to Christ. The question we'll tackle in this element—*The Life*—is whether we represent Him well to those watching or leave them utterly unconvinced.

INSIDE OUT

In 2 Corinthians 5:20, Paul says we are *". . .Christ's ambassadors, as though God were making his appeal through us."* Not only has our identity been changed from enemies of God *(Col. 1:21)* to adopted sons and daughters *(Rom. 8:14-15)*, but also representatives, delegates, and spokespeople of the Savior of the universe. The implications of that statement are massive. We've been saved, transformed, and called to live lives on display for the world to see and give glory to God *(1 Peter 2:12)*.

Notice how the first three elements of an outward-focused life work together seamlessly—the gospel leads to changed hearts, changed hearts lead to changed lives, and changed lives point others to Christ. The connection between our hearts and lives can't be overstated. They harmonize with one another, for good or for bad. Jesus highlights this relationship for us while debating with a group of Pharisees who are convinced He is casting out demons by the power of Beelzebul, the prince of demons.

> *You brood of vipers, how can you who are evil say anything good? For the mouth speaks what the heart is full of. A good man brings good things out of the good stored up in him, and an evil man brings evil things out of the evil stored up in him. (Matt. 12:34-35)*

Or in other words, what's going on in your heart *will* come out of your mouth. Like a pot left boiling on the stove, our thoughts, desires, and beliefs overflow into the world around us. I like to explain the bond between our hearts and lives by using two reciprocal phrases and a simple drawing.

- What I believe *determines* how I live.
- How I live *reveals* what I believe.

No one can see what's going on inside your heart and mind—what you believe. There's a giant shield in the way. I can't peer into your heart to understand your relationship with God any more than I can guess your favorite band or dessert. There's no way for me to experience your faith and beliefs the way you do. They are a complete mystery to me. I'm on the outside looking in.

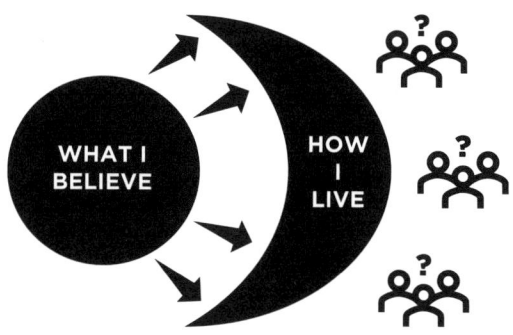

The only way I could possibly see what's happening on the inside is through your lifestyle: your actions, words, and priorities. Even silly things like your facial expressions open the window into your heart. This might seem elementary, but it's a monumentally important part of our role as Christ's ambassadors.

Evangelism is an *outward action* determined by *inward belief*. It's rooted in what we believe about God, not just the words we say. However, just because it begins internally doesn't mean it stays there. Our understanding of the gospel, story of transformation, and intimacy with Jesus keep us spiritually healthy and ready to reach others, but it's the way we *live* that shows those on the outside what we believe and if we've truly been changed by God. Philosopher and theologian, Dallas Willard, uses this example.

> Mahatma Gandhi, who had looked closely at Christianity as practiced around him in Great Britain, remarked that if only Christians would live according to their belief in the teachings of Jesus, "we all would become Christians." We know what he meant, and he was right in that. But the dismaying truth is that the Christians were living according to their "belief" in the teachings of Jesus. They didn't believe them!
>
> Moreover, knowing the "right answers"... does not mean we believe them. To believe them, like believing anything else, means that we are set to act as if they (the right answers) are true and that we will do so in appropriate circumstances. And acting as if the right answers are true means, in turn, that we intend to obey the example and teachings of Jesus the Anointed.[4]

SOMEBODY'S WATCHING ME

People *are* watching, by the way. Neighbors, family members, classmates, employees, and complete strangers are constantly making observations about the way believers live. Sometimes it's out of openminded curiosity or a quest to find hope, and sometimes it's more cynical—a smug game of "*Gotcha!*" pointing out the shortcomings of those who dare to wear the badge of Christianity. Either way, we are ambassadors, representing the Lord whether we like it or not.

I'm never more aware of this fact than when I head to the

---

4   Dallas Willard, *Renovation of the Heart: Putting on the Character of Christ - 20th Anniversary Edition*. (Colorado: NavPress, 2021), 86, Kindle

store for a late-night pint of ice cream. It's tempting to think I can fade into the background, but just think of all the little ways my pajama-clad trip could impact others.

Will I be patient as I drive through the crowded parking lot? Should I return the shopping cart for the mom buckling her kids into their car seats? Will I drop a dollar into the Salvation Army bucket or be kind to the Girl Scouts selling cookies out front? Will I exchange friendly nods with others or avoid eye contact entirely? Finally, will I offer the teenage cashier a smile, asking about her day, or will I hold my breath, hoping she doesn't comment on my attire?

Each day is filled with little choices—moments on display inviting others to make assumptions about our lives, and more importantly, our God. A simple trip to the grocery store could paint me as a saint or indict me as a villain in someone else's story. But if it's true that what I believe about God determines how I live, I already have answers to all these questions. Let's run it again.

If I believe God created me, loves me, sent His Son to die in my place so I can be with Him forever, and *if* I believe He has called me to live His way and tell others about Him, my little trip becomes an opportunity. My patience in the parking lot is intentional because I want to honor the safety and value of others. I cheerfully offer to return the shopping cart, knowing it's only a fraction of the kindness and selflessness afforded to me by Christ. I can be generous with my money and time because they, too, are gifts from God. I meet the gaze of anyone who might need a smile or some hope at the end of a tough day, and I approach my cashier full and overflowing, looking to pour into others. Being rooted in the gospel and remembering my identity in Christ leads me to a life that is surrendered to Him and excited about His mission.

But that's only half of the lifestyle equation—our half. One of the key pieces to understanding *The Life's* role in evangelism is considering the perspective and perceptions of those on the outside. Let's replay our little scenario one final time, but this time, look through the lens of what *others* see.

The elderly couple making their way slowly across the parking lot, feeling guilty for not moving faster, look up to see a soft smile and gentle gesture communicating, "Take your time. I'm in no rush."

The mom, frustrated and overwhelmed after saying no to the endless bombardment of small-voiced requests and stressed by the thought of leaving her kids unsupervised to return her cart is touched by the kindness of a stranger.

Both the bell-wielding Santa and the sharply dressed Girl Scout are thankful, excited to take one more step toward their goal.

Employees in the aisles are overjoyed to be treated like people instead of annoyances as they stock the shelves, and the teenage cashier, struggling silently with fear, worry, and hopelessness, is encouraged by a customer using her name, making her smile, and asking if she needs prayer. How we live reveals what we believe to others.

This type of intentional outward-focused living is not always at the forefront of our minds. We don't realize how many people need what we have and how our every action either draws them closer to Christ or pushes them further away. We are His ambassadors, a delegation from heaven sent to represent the light of the world to those wandering in darkness.

COUNTING THE COST

I married the love of my life on January 11, 2014 at the ripe old age of twenty-two. I had yet to finish my undergraduate degree, move out of my dorm room, or achieve financial autonomy from my parents, whereas my wife had her own home, three dogs, and a master's degree. Yes, I understand I married up. My nights were spent playing Ping-Pong and watching movies while she did adult things like paying taxes and changing the oil in her car. To say my life changed on January 11, 2014 is an understatement.

I ceased being a fiancé and became a husband. Suddenly, I wasn't only responsible for *my* life, but someone else's. Bills needed paying, dogs needed walking, and meals needed cooking. I entered into a beautiful and fulfilling world that my wife had created, but I didn't just get to sit back and enjoy it—we were now partners in it. Gone were the days of 3am Ping-Pong. I bade farewell to late-night video game binges fueled by Mountain Dew. Instead, I settled into bed at 9pm, setting my alarm so I could wake up, help my wife make breakfast, and get to school before a full day of work.

Looking back on this scene from a decade ago brings a smile to my face, but not because I necessarily enjoyed it. It was hard work. I'll be honest. The shift from bachelor to husband was jarring. Many young men are terrified of crossing over into domestication, seeing the bills, chores, and responsibility as shackles keeping fun and freedom out of reach.

No, I didn't love every moment. But I *do* love my wife. I love her more than any game, friendship, or freedom that came before her. And so, with a dopey, lovestruck smile on my face, I mowed the grass. I went to work daydreaming of the moment I would walk through the door of *our* home. And every morning as I slipped my finger into the cold metal of my wedding ring, I would remember how my life had radically changed with two simple words—"I do"—and I would happily get to work all over again.

This story could easily have a different ending, couldn't it? I've spoken with numerous couples as they recount the very same marital tasks with anger, hurt, and bitterness. Words like "have to" describe what was once "get to"—the responsibilities that began in love now fanning the flame of resentment.

Others view their newfound relationship as license to kick back and enjoy all the benefits of their spouse's love without sharing any of the burden. Don't believe me? Watch a sitcom. How many times have we seen the aloof husband kick back with a beer and some uninterrupted football after a long day at the office while his wife frantically wrangles kids and cooks dinner, all while looking her best?

What's fascinating is that in each scenario, the *tasks* necessary for a successful marriage and fulfilled life remain the same. Bills need paying, cars need washing, and meals need cooking. So, what makes the outcomes so different?

The value placed on the relationship. Is this person—this relationship—*worth* my sacrifice and effort? When I think of my wife, my answer is a resounding yes! In fact, I've built my entire life around my new identity, not only as a husband, but now a father of two—and no one prepared me for how much sacrifice *that* would take.

COST OF DISCIPLESHIP

Jesus gave us a sneak peek into what a relationship with Him entails in Mark 8 when He said,

> *Whoever wants to be my disciple must deny themselves and take up their cross and follow me. For whoever wants to save their life will lose it, but whoever loses their life for me and for the gospel will save it. (vv. 34-35)*

That's a little more intense than some dishes and laundry, if you ask me. Following Jesus means handing the authority of *every* decision and priority to Him. To many, the thought of giving God complete control is not only terrifying, but the very thing keeping them from a relationship with Him in the first place. Like the teenage boy who can't fathom *why* any man in his right mind would happily do dishes and change diapers, it's a struggle for those far from Christ to understand the joy of Christian obedience.

But they're not alone. I believe many professing *Christians* struggle to truly understand that joy, and by doing so, render themselves completely ineffective in God's mission to reach the lost.

CHEAP VS COSTLY

In his book, *The Cost of Discipleship*, theologian Dietrich Bonhoeffer introduces us to cheap and costly grace, two views of Christ's sacrifice that lead to radically different lifestyles. I love these words because they communicate value. Just like our marriage example, we must ask ourselves the question, "Is Christ *worth* my own personal sacrifice and effort?" If we're rooted in the gospel and regularly reflecting on how He has transferred us from the domain of darkness to the kingdom of Christ *(Col. 1:13)*, our answer to that question should be obvious. However, if we've neglected the gospel, taken Christ's sacrifice for granted, or fooled ourselves into thinking we're better off on our own, things get messy pretty quickly.

First, let's talk about *cheap grace*—accepting God's gift of salvation with no cost to me or the way I live. Bonhoeffer puts it this way:

> Cheap grace means the justification of the sin without the justification of the sinner. Grace alone does everything, they say, and so everything can remain as it was before. . . . [It] is the preaching of forgiveness without requiring repentance.[5]

Simply put, this attitude toward God's gift is flippant, dismissive, and entitled. "Oh, Jesus died on the cross so I don't have to pay for my own sins? How convenient for me! I can live any way I want because I don't have to pay the bill." Like a miserable spouse, cheap-grace Christians fail to understand the beauty of sacrifice and, in doing so, miss out on the joy of obedience.

---
5 Dietrich Bonhoeffer, *The Cost of Discipleship* (New York: Simon and Schuster, 1995), 44

Bonhoeffer contrasts this cheap, empty view of God's grace by highlighting *costly grace*—the invaluable worth of Christ's sacrifice and the effect it has on all those who see it rightly.

> Costly grace is the treasure in the field; for the sake of it a man will gladly go and sell all that he has (Matt. 13:44). It is the pearl of great price to buy which the merchant will sell all his goods (Matt. 13:45-46). It is the kingly rule of Christ, for whose sake a man will pluck out the eye which causes him to stumble (Mark 9:47); it is the call of Jesus Christ at which the disciple leaves his nets and follows Him (Matt. 4:20). . . . Grace is costly because it compels a man to submit to the yoke of Christ and follow Him; it is grace because Jesus says, "My yoke is easy and my burden is light" (Matt. 11:29).[6]

What we believe about God will either allow us to live like the world or cause us to live in submission to Christ. One is a great harm to our witness; the other is a great help. The value we ascribe to Him determines how joyfully and eagerly we obey, and how effective we are in our evangelistic efforts.

POBODY'S NERFECT

I know what you're thinking. "If the way I live has such a huge impact on my ability to effectively share my faith, I'm toast!" Trust me, I've been there, too. It can be tempting, especially after Bonhoeffer's explanation of cheap and costly

---

[6] Dietrich Bonhoeffer, *The Cost of Discipleship* (New York: Simon and Schuster, 1995), 45

grace, to think that perfection is required to make disciples. And so, knowing that we fall far short of God's standard, we begin to rationalize why we're unqualified or unneeded in His mission.

This is a fairly normal reaction. In fact, most every time I discuss this element, I see wheels turn and shoulders slump as people put two and two together. We think, "I mess up. I sin, sometimes on purpose. I must be a cheap-grace Christian. God would never use someone like me."

Be careful, though. The enemy wants nothing more than for you to disqualify yourself and stay quiet. The reason we fall for it so easily is because, like most of his lies, there's an element of truth at play. Those who live openly sinful lives *will* struggle to effectively reach others with the gospel. Rejecting God's authority and direction leads to Christians being unconvincing ambassadors. Both of these statements ring true. But notice how craftily the enemy twists these truths into indictments leveled at anyone who sins *at all*. Suddenly, we're drowning in a works-based theology of perfection. Sneaky, isn't he?

This is why it's so important to be rooted in the gospel. If our foundation is weak, our application will topple. However, the enemy's accusations evaporate in the minds of those who understand the true essence of the gospel message—that we are *unable* to be perfect, but Christ substituted His perfection in our place. Then, and only then, we are redeemed and changed to be more like Him every day.

One of my favorite passages in the Bible is found in the letter of 1 John.

> *If we claim to be without sin, we deceive ourselves and the truth is not in us. If we confess our sins, he is faithful and just and will forgive us our sins and purify us from all unrighteousness. If we claim we have not sinned, we make him out to be a liar and his word is not in us.* (1 John 1:8-10)

Follow the logic. We sin, even after being redeemed and given a new heart. Anyone who says he *doesn't* sin is a liar and has bigger things to worry about. But here's where it gets really incredible. God is so personal and so good that He invites us to approach Him with our sin, confess it, and receive His limitless forgiveness. Every time we approach Him in repentance, He wipes our sin away, making it as if it never happened. But John's not done yet! Check out what he says in the very next section.

> *My dear children, I write this to you so that you will not sin. But if anybody does sin, we have an advocate with the Father—Jesus Christ, the Righteous One. He is the atoning sacrifice for our sins, and not only for ours but also for the sins of the whole world.* (1 John 2:1-2)

He says, "You sin. You mess up. That's a fact. The good news is that God is faithful to forgive! Don't get me wrong, though. Do everything you can to *avoid* sin. But when you inevitably screw up again. . . look to Jesus, confess, and be forgiven."

Isn't that incredible? It's right there in God's Word! Our lives as believers are not defined by perfection, but by the value we place on Christ and the urgency with which we run to Him in times of trouble. The biggest difference between those who dismiss God's grace as cheap and those who value it as costly is repentance. Costly grace doesn't mean we'll be perfect, but that we'll joyfully and eagerly surrender our imperfections to God as we grow steadily in Christlikeness. Understanding this simple concept frees us from performance-based faith and allows us to point to a good God, even when we miss the mark.

OBJECTIVE PERSPECTIVE

Let's end this discussion where it all began, by asking ourselves if our lives reflect what we claim to believe. When people see the way we live—our decisions, priorities, and reactions—will they be drawn closer to Christ or alienated from Him?

I like to consider a few introspective questions as I work through this element. First, how does my lifestyle *confirm* what I say I believe? What *positive* behaviors do people see when they look at me? I often pray before I eat, no matter where I am. I sacrifice my Sunday mornings to spend time at church. It might not seem like much, but simple Christian rhythms and habits can speak volumes to those looking for peace, hope, or meaning. Take a few moments to ponder how your lifestyle confirms your witness.

You can probably guess what's coming next. If we're going to list the positive, it might also be important to consider how our lives *contradict* what we say we believe. Personally, I have to be on guard against sarcasm and humor at the wrong times or at the expense of others. Nothing shatters my witness more than a hurtful, albeit clever, joke.

It's also helpful to put ourselves in the shoes of others to get a 30,000-foot view of our lives. After all, perception is often as concrete as reality for many people. I ask myself, "If the non-Christians in my life were asked to describe my lifestyle, what might they say?" How would others sum up *your* life? Phew... that's a gut check to think about! Or we could take it one step further and ask, "If I asked that same group to describe my *faith*, what might they say?" When pursuing an outward-focused life, it's incredibly helpful to consider the perspectives of those on the outside looking in.

ANOTHER TOOL IN THE BELT

So, are we unconvincing ambassadors or illuminated illustrations of the gospel? There is so much more to be said about our growth as children of God, but let's keep our eyes focused outward. When we understand our role as Christ's representatives, see the connection between belief and action, value a relationship with God above all else, and regularly surrender our shortcomings to Him, our lives become powerful instruments to reach the lost.

ASK YOURSELF

- Why is it important for my life to reflect my beliefs?
- How has my lifestyle confirmed or contradicted what I claim to believe?
- Are there are behaviors I need to surrender before trying to reach others with the gospel?

Element Four
THE LOST

Am I motivated to reach others?

MOTIVATION MATTERS

I remember stepping on the scale a few years ago and not liking the number I saw. Apparently, working in student ministry surrounded by cheap pizza and pumpkin spice lattes isn't great for the ol' waistline. It was diet time.

My days began to revolve around losing weight. Sugary lattes became boring cups of black coffee, I squeezed in pushups between meetings, and I never missed my hydration goal of a gallon each day. I was motivated with laser focus. I *had* to lose weight. But as my body changed physically, something also changed mentally. One of the mantras I recited to myself was, "If it brings me joy, I can't eat it." Food was fuel and nothing more. I began to make nutritional decisions based on things I had heard, piecing together my own health science; and it wasn't long before I started to hate food, working out, and even the progress I had made. Resentment washed over me every time I got onto the exercise bike or opened *another* can of tuna.

Sure, I was doing what I set out to do, but I had no energy or mental sharpness. My body screamed for carbohydrates, fats, and calories, only to be fed more protein. I was miserable and exhausted.

See, I didn't care about being healthy—just losing weight. My actions and habits were completely out of whack, but, on a much deeper level, my *motives* were unhealthy, unbalanced, and dangerous to myself and others.

My fitness journey would have been completely different if I had stopped to ask the question "*Why* do I want to lose weight?" before jumping into endless hours of cardio. Calibrating my motivation would have likely revealed the best way to approach diet, exercise, and long-term health. Why did I want to lose weight? Well, I was tired all the time. Despite being young, I struggled to get on the floor and play with my kids. I wasn't sleeping well. I wanted to live long enough to raise a family. I wanted to be healthy and full of energy. And yes, I wanted my pants to fit again.

Balance. Go ahead and diet, but carbs and fats are important. Exercise is key, but too much will cause damage.

Rest days are important both mentally and physically. Calibrated, healthy motivation leads to lasting change.

The same can be said about evangelism. There are various reasons we *should* share the gospel but stopping to ask *why* and understanding the full picture are crucial to remaining healthy and excited about reaching our fourth element—*The Lost*.

GOD'S MISSION

In the last chapter of Matthew, we find one of the clearest passages in the entire Bible about evangelism—the Great Commission.

> *Then Jesus came to them and said, "All authority in heaven and on earth has been given to me. Therefore go and make disciples of all nations, baptizing them in the name of the Father and of the Son and of the Holy Spirit, and teaching them to obey everything I have commanded you. And surely I am with you always, to the very end of the age." (Matt. 28-18-20)*

This passage is just one of many that highlight the first reason we share the gospel—and it's a big one. *God literally told us to.* He has a mission—go make disciples—and He calls us to play a part in that mission. Those who hear the gospel, repent, surrender, and live as ambassadors of Christ likely aren't shocked by these marching orders. In this case, our *obedience* to an almighty God is what motivates us to get in the game.

OUR PURPOSE

To understand the second primary reason for evangelism, think back to the very beginning of Scripture—to the book of Genesis. What was the intended purpose of man? Why were we created? Well, we already covered it when we discussed the gospel. We were created to be in a loving relationship with God. Or, as the *Westminster Shorter Catechism* puts it, "Man's chief end is to glorify God, and to enjoy Him forever."[7]

Jesus echoed the intention of Genesis and the words of Deuteronomy and Leviticus when asked what God desires most from His people—our purpose.

> "Teacher, which is the greatest commandment in the Law?" Jesus replied: "'Love the Lord your God with all your heart and with all your soul and with all your mind.' This is the first and greatest commandment. And the second is like it: 'Love your neighbor as yourself.' All the Law and the Prophets hang on these two commandments." (Matt. 22:36-40)

Love God and love others—in that order. We don't just share the gospel because God told us to. We do it because pursuing Him with everything we have—heart, soul, and mind—develops intimacy with Him, and if you've been taking notes, you'll remember that intimacy with God naturally motivates us to impact others. Seeking the Lord each day opens our eyes to see others as He does, not through the lens of our fallen, human, inward-focused worldview.

---

7   Edwin Hall, *The Shorter Catechism of the Westminster Assembly with Analysis and Scripture Proofs* (Philadelphia: Presbyterian Publication Committee, 1859), 5

THE LOST

When we remember His grace, mercy, and sacrifice, loving our neighbors becomes an overflow, not just cold obedience.

We love because he first loved us. (1 John 4:19)

THEIR NEED

The third reason we share the gospel might not be as clear-cut as obedience to God's mission or as simple as "love God, love people," but it is just as important. The spiritual need of others is the helpful negative motivation we must remember as we wake up each morning.

What does the Bible say about our spiritual state again? Oh, that's right.

> ...for all have sinned and fall short of the glory of God. (Rom. 3:23)

> ...sin entered the world through one man, and death through sin, and in this way death came to all people, because all sinned... (Rom. 5:12)

> ...for the wages of sin is death... (Rom. 6:23a)

Any questions? We're motivated to reach the lost because they are separated from God and still ruled by sin. The word *urgency* comes to mind. We urgently reach others because we know the need, we know the stakes, and we know just how good the other side is.

KEEPING OUR BALANCE

Let's put it all together. God invites us into His mission to seek and save the lost, He calls us to love Him with everything we have—overflowing into those around us—and He reminds us of the overwhelming need of those far from Him. When held together in harmony, these three reasons properly motivate us to obey, love, and move with urgency.

But what happens when one aspect is minimized, overemphasized, or left out completely? Well, much like a car missing a wheel, things get bumpy.

> Obedience + Love − Urgency = No Rush
> Urgency + Obedience − Love = No Grace
> Love + Urgency − Obedience = No Gospel

It doesn't matter how much we focus on God's mission and our purpose to love others; without urgency we will simply be in no rush. How many of us are waiting around for the *perfect* moment to come along or think we have all the time in the world when, in reality, we've forgotten the weight of people's separation from God?

At the same time, overemphasizing the spiritual need of others can lead to an obsession with *closing the deal* or *doing whatever it takes* to ensure salvation, even cheapening or changing the gospel to make it more alluring.

Knowing God's mission and the spiritual need of others but ignoring our purpose—to love God and love people—will lead to a jarring lack of grace. In this scenario, evangelism becomes an obligation rather than an overflow.

But watch out! Focusing too much on our purpose can lead to inward-focused faith—always feeling the need to spend a little more time loving people and loving God, but never taking the bold step to share the gospel. Relationships are important, as we've already discussed, but at some point our love for others must lead to gospel conversations.

Finally, being confident in our purpose and understanding the spiritual need of others but minimizing the part we play in God's mission will rob *others* of hearing the gospel. Without obedience, good intentions replace action and follow-through. Much like my fitness journey, overemphasizing obedience can lead to things like spiritual burnout and resentment. Blind obedience separated from a loving relationship with God and genuine love for others is unsustainable.

GETTING BACK ON THE BEAM

The specific reasons we share the gospel are influenced heavily by our context. Past experiences and interpersonal relationships play a big role in defining our *"why,"* but so do the messages we hear in sermons, books, movies, and other media. I have heard many sermons unpacking the Great Commission, but they aren't the same sermons you've heard. I've read both helpful and unhelpful books about sharing my faith, and don't even get me started on the endless stream of theological musings posted online.

Our motivation is slowly cultivated through various moments, voices, and conclusions—pieces of a puzzle working together to form our image of evangelism. That picture can be complete and beautiful, or skewed and confusing, but one thing is certain: Unbalanced motivation doesn't happen overnight; it happens slowly over time.

However, much like the *check engine* light in your car, recognizing this imbalance is simply an indicator that something needs to be addressed. Calibrating evangelistic motivation is a lifelong process. Instead of disqualifying yourself from God's mission because you notice that your *why* is unbalanced, take it to the Lord.

The best way to healthily balance God's mission, our purpose, and the spiritual need of others is prayer. Surrendering our ambitions and desires the Lord and asking for His wisdom and guidance is the quickest way to achieve harmony. After surrendering our motives to Him, we can open His Word to receive a clear, thorough response and see the whole picture.

Before you move on, pause, and ask yourself, "What motivates me to share the gospel? Am I balanced or unbalanced? What do I need to surrender to God to recalibrate my *why*?"

RED CARS

Once we've spent some time contemplating and surrendering *why* we share the gospel, it's finally time to turn our focus toward others. I'm aware that I've spent an incredible number of pages talking about you—your understanding of the gospel, your heart, your life, and your motivation. Isn't this a book about evangelism? We have to talk about other people eventually, right? Well, you're exactly right, but I hope you see how important our vertical relationship with God is before we begin to look horizontally at others. If evangelism is truly an overflow, like I keep claiming, filling up is critical; but now that we've done that, let's talk about *The Lost*.

I like to use this example whenever I talk to Christians about the people in their lives who don't know Christ. "How many red cars did you pass last time you went to church?" Usually, I'll get some smarty-pants who gives me an exact number, to which I say, "Liar!" Whether you're reading this on a Sunday afternoon or Friday evening, whether you live six blocks from church or forty-five minutes away, you have no idea how many red cars you passed. You know red cars exist, you know they're out on the road or parked in driveways, and you know you probably passed at least one, but you can't say for sure how many. Why? Because you weren't paying attention.

Jesus had an amazing propensity to *notice* people. In contrast, I'm often so wrapped up in my own little world that I pass by people completely unaware that they need hope. It's not that I'm uninterested; it's that I'm not paying attention. Not Jesus, though. He *saw* people, no matter where He went. He stopped, looked them in the eyes, and injected the good news of God's kingdom into their situation. The Gospels—Matthew, Mark, Luke, and John—are full of examples of Jesus noticing the red cars.

SPHERE OF INFLUENCE

What I find so fascinating is the *way* Jesus noticed people. He's walking next to the Sea of Galilee? "Oh look, fishermen! Come follow me and I will make you fishers of men!" *(Matt. 4:18-20)*. He needs a drink at a well? "Why don't I ask this Samaritan woman and strike up a conversation about living water?" *(John 4:5-26)*. Jesus recognized the people in His sphere of influence. And He's given us the same gift.

Here's an easy way to start finding red cars in your own life. First, think about *proximity*—the people *near* you on a regular basis: neighbors, coworkers, your children; or if you're a kid, your parents! God put those people in your life.

Next, consider *regularity*—people you see *often*. Do you

run into the same lady walking her dog every morning? Have you considered the person you sit next to in math class, the person you share an office with, or someone on your soccer team? God gives us opportunity after opportunity to impact others.

Finally, *commonality*. What do you like to do? What are your hobbies? Are you a Fantasy Football nut or country music fan? Are you part of a book club? God made you unique, but the things you're drawn to also draw others. We have an opportunity to impact *like-minded* people—people we would never encounter if not for our hobbies and interests.

Part of living an outward-focused life is seeing through the eyes of Christ, looking beyond our needs, wants, and obligations, and noticing the people God brings across our path every day.

NOTICING NEIGHBORS

Let's pivot. The red car example is great (if I do say so myself), but I think Jesus used a better word. When talking about our horizontal relationship with people, He said, "Love your *neighbor* as yourself." But what does He mean by neighbor? Well, we're not the first ones to ask that question.

In Luke 10:25-37, a religious leader asked Jesus, *"Who is my neighbor?"* to which He responded by telling the story of the Good Samaritan. It goes like this. A Jewish man was beaten, robbed, and left to die on the side of the road. Two other Jewish men, a priest then a Levite, came across the scene, but passed by him without stopping to help. Finally, a Samaritan, someone who, according to this religious leader, had no business helping the wounded man, stopped and cared for him. He took him to an inn and paid for his recovery. The passage concludes with Jesus asking the inquisitive religious leader,

> *"Which of these three do you think was a neighbor to the man who fell into the hands of robbers?" (v. 36).*

Jesus' point here is that our neighbor is not just the person from our *tribe*—the one who looks like us, acts like us, or thinks like us. It is anyone who needs the hope, mercy, grace, and love of Christ.

As we labor to notice red cars, let's change our vocabulary. Let's notice neighbors. Who are the people God has placed in our lives who need what we have?

Scripture calls us the light of the world *(Matt. 5:14-16)*, a royal priesthood *(1 Peter 2:9)*, and ambassadors of Christ *(2 Cor. 5:20)*. Those are all incredibly *active* words. Light shines, priests point to God, and ambassadors represent.

We are called to champion God's message of hope to those stuck in darkness, but it all means nothing if we don't take the time to notice and move toward our neighbors. What good is a candle in a well-lit room or an ambassador in his home country? Living an outward-focused life requires us to leave the safety and comfort of what's *known* to impact what's *needed*.

WELL, WHADDYA KNOW?

And because these neighbors are people, not projects, we don't just pay attention to each person's spiritual state, but their story. Genuinely listening to the stories, experiences, and opinions of others is incredibly helpful when determining how to share the gospel most effectively. I like to ask myself some questions to see how much or how little I know about the people God has put in my life.

First, how long have I known them? What's our history together? How do I know them?

Next, I spend some time thinking about their faith background. Do I know how they grew up? Do I know if they believe in God or understand anything about Christianity? Am I talking nonsense when I quote Scripture or did they go to church when they were younger?

Do I have any idea what opinions they have about faith? Are they cynical? Are they apathetic? Why do they feel the way they do? Have I ever interacted with these people about faith? Do they know *I'm* a Christian?

Okay, now picture someone in your sphere of influence—a specific person with a face—and go back through those questions... How'd you do? How much do you know?

It's a humbling exercise sometimes as I realize just how surface-level my relationships are with those far from Christ. However, no need to despair, because like so much of the material in this book, now that I know where I am, I can begin taking next steps to grow!

GET CURIOUS

One of the most practical things I can say about this element is also one of the most basic. If we want to reach other people with the gospel, we have to get curious. We have to ask questions, listen intently, remember details, and love genuinely. But be warned: Your curiosity will reveal things that are uncomfortable. People *will* talk to you about what they believe, but it may not be pleasant to hear the faith you hold dear dragged through the mud by people who have been hurt by cheap-grace Christians or churches.

This is why we must be rooted in the gospel. It's why we stay close to Christ—because in Him we have everything we need. We don't need the approval of others; we don't need them to agree with us. We can humbly absorb accusations and respond with love. We can be patient and merciful when our convictions are attacked because we see the big picture and understand that people won't care what we know until they know that we care.

Let me be clear about something, though. Care does not mean condone. I've had heartbreaking conversations with Christians who refuse to interact with certain people because of the way they live or what they believe. They are paralyzed by the fear that loving such people will be misconstrued as approval of their lifestyle. In these moments, I like to gently remind my brothers and sisters in Christ that just because I treat individuals with dignity, love, and gentleness does not mean I am celebrating their decisions. And for those struggling with this concept, the answer is simple—spend some time reading Matthew, Mark, Luke, and

John. Take note of all the times Jesus moved *toward* those the religious elite condemned and avoided, and ask yourself the age-old question: What would Jesus do?

We're putting all this work into living an outward-focused life because we want *more* for people. We want them to know Christ, but it's often a process, and our loving curiosity will reveal the best way to inject hope into the lives of those who need it.

LIGHT TO THE LOST

By now, things should be clicking. So many people begin by focusing on the lost, but because their own light is dim, dampened by unbalanced motivation, sinful living, distance from God, or a misunderstanding of the gospel, they find it hard to consistently live on mission. But when we take time to cultivate each element, humbly surrendering to God each step of the way, we can shine brightly in a world shrouded in darkness.

ASK YOURSELF

- When it comes to sharing my faith, what motivates me most?
- Why should my motivation be balanced? *Is* my motivation balanced?
- How many people do I regularly interact with who need to hear the gospel? How much do I know about what they believe?

Element Five
THE GAP

Am I hesitant to share the gospel?

NOT SO FAST

Element Five is a tricky one. It sneaks up on us right as we're starting to get excited. Follow the logic.

> If I am rooted in the gospel. . .
> If I remember how my heart has been transformed. . .
> If my life reflects what I claim to believe. . .
> And if I am motivated to reach others. . .
> Sharing the gospel should be easy!

So why isn't it? I'll use a quick example from my short career as a middle school basketball player. I knew, even at eleven years old, how to dribble a basketball, which direction I should run, and the mechanics of a basic layup, but every time I had the opportunity to score, I froze. My legs stopped working, I forgot how to bounce a ball, and the hoop suddenly seemed thirty feet in the air. I knew the basics, but quickly learned that my understanding of the game didn't guarantee my execution in the moment.

We may know the gospel, know people who need to hear it, and have every intention of sharing it, but when we finally get an opportunity to put it all together—we freeze.

I love pointing to my lackluster athletic experience when introducing this concept because it's exactly how many Christians have experienced evangelism. Moments came and went, conversations turned awkward, and we learned to avoid spiritual things. We were conditioned to stay quiet. And instead of investigating *why* we hesitate, we quit, often hanging our head in shame—feeling like we had let God down.

I didn't recognize it in the moment, but looking back a couple decades, I can tell you why I froze. I didn't want to let my team down. Despite wearing the jersey, I didn't feel all that confident in my ability to do what seemed so easy for others. So, after two years of feeling like an imposter on my own team, I quit.

Ask yourself this element's question, "Am I hesitant to share the gospel," but don't stop there. Dig a little deeper, and ask, "*Why* am I hesitant? What stops me?" I like to use a specific term to describe our many responses to questions like these—I call them *gospel gaps*.

THE GOSPEL GAP

A gospel gap is anything that stops us from sharing the good news of Jesus. Think of this gap like a chasm between two cliffs. One cliff is *knowledge*—knowing the gospel and those who need to hear it. The other cliff is *action*—actually moving toward others and sharing what we know about Jesus.

The only way to move from knowledge to action is by recognizing our gaps—fears, hesitations, and lies from the enemy—and filling them with God's truth.

DIALECTS AND ROOTS

It is so easy, in this discussion, to feel singled out and alone. Much like seventh grade Andrew watching other kids make shot after shot, we think, "I am the only one who struggles to share the gospel. . ."

In 2020, I put together a little survey and sent it to hundreds of people from various ages, backgrounds, denominations, ethnicities, countries, and levels of spiritual maturity. I wanted to know what was keeping people from sharing their faith, and after a couple months, I had a list of a few hundred gaps. You can probably imagine the spread. Some people wrote novels to fully articulate their reasoning while others used a single word. Then came the fun part—the spreadsheet! As I carefully examined each answer, I noticed something amazing. A pattern emerged.

Think of it this way. When I see you, I could greet you by saying "Hello," "Hey," "Hi," "Yo," "Greetings," or various other salutations. I can express the same root sentiment in many ways. These unique ways are often referred to as *dialects*.

I realized, while looking at the survey data, that many of the answers seemed to be saying the same thing—unique dialects stemming from the same roots. For example:

DIALECT 1: "I'm anxious it will harm my relationships."
DIALECT 2: "I don't want to push people away."
DIALECT 3: "Talking about faith makes people upset."

ROOT GAP: Fear of offending

As you can see, three people used different words based on unique experiences with various individuals to say the same thing. *"I'm afraid that I'll offend someone."* So it went with the hundreds of gaps I received. I meticulously categorized them until each dialect found its root, and when I finished, I was left with seven gospel gaps. Seven. Not 1,393. Not one for every person on the planet. There were seven root gaps shared by every believer who has ever hesitated to share the good news.

We all have unique reasons for staying silent, and we express them in various ways, but tracing our individual gap dialects down to their roots can bring great comfort, confidence, and community as we realize gaps are normal, they can be overcome, and we're not alone.

Let's spend a few pages walking through these seven roots, turning to God's Word to help us. If we believe that Scripture is all-sufficient, we can trust it to help us not only understand and navigate our gaps but overcome them once and for all.

FEAR OF REJECTION

No one likes to be rejected. I went to high school. I know how this works. It's much easier to change my behavior to *fit in* than it is to risk rejection. The fear of rejection causes us to remain silent to preserve our relationships or reputation.

- What if they turn me down and things get weird?
- What if they label me, call me names, or spread rumors about me?

This gap is so ferocious that it can cause us to compromise our convictions, hide our identity, and pledge our allegiance to the crowd over the King. But what does Scripture have to say about navigating rejection? Take a look at what Jesus told His disciples.

> *If the world hates you, keep in mind that it hated me first. If you belonged to the world, it would love you as its own.*

> *As it is, you do not belong to the world, but I have chosen you out of the world. That is why the world hates you. (John 15:18-19)*

I want nothing more than to be like Jesus. I want to act like Him, think like Him, respond like Him, and speak like Him. And yet, despite my desire to imitate Him in all things, I often shudder at the thought of being *treated* like Him.

You don't have to read much of the New Testament to see that Jesus was rejected. He was beaten, betrayed, abandoned, humiliated, and crucified. He was rejected to the highest degree, but instead of running from the adversity and hardship that comes with our faith, we're called to take up our cross and follow Him *(Mark 8:31-38)*.

It's in these dark moments of fear that I cling to examples like Paul, a man who took Christ's invitation seriously and was rewarded by being rejected, hunted, beaten, jailed, and beheaded. And yet, as he sat in prison, charged of nothing other than preaching the gospel, he penned these words.

> *I know what it is to be in need, and I know what it is to have plenty. I have learned the secret of being content in any and every situation, whether well fed or hungry, whether living in plenty or in want. I can do all this through him who gives me strength. (Phil. 4:12-13)*

I believe Jesus meant it when He said,

> *Blessed are you when people insult you, persecute you and falsely say all kinds of evil against you because of me. Re-*

joice and be glad, because great is your reward in Heaven. (Matt. 5:11-12a)

If our goal is to imitate Jesus, we can rejoice when we're treated like Him. I can't promise you less rejection. But I can remind you that rejection by a fallen world is evidence that you belong to God. After all, this is not our final destination. We're just passing through on our way home.

FEAR OF INADEQUACY

Maybe you're not as worried about being rejected as you are about looking foolish. The fear of inadequacy is our second gospel gap root—remaining silent due to a perceived lack of ability or understanding. Let those *qualified* Christians share the gospel—the pastors, elders, and missionaries.

- What if I forget something or mess up?
- What if they ask me questions and I don't have all the answers?

Remember when I said the gospel is beautiful in its simplicity? God is so good that He doesn't require us to have complete and perfect knowledge—just to be willing, obedient, and in love with Him. I like the way Paul says it in his letter to the philosophy-dominated Corinthians.

> *. . . [Christ sent me] to preach the gospel—not with wisdom and eloquence, lest the cross of Christ be emptied of its power. (1 Cor. 1:17)*

ALWAYS GOING

Paul could have held his own in a philosophical debate about gospel-adjacent doctrines, but he knew that the beauty and power of the gospel are its simplicity and accessibility to anyone willing to surrender.

There's a saying around my church—a sort of motto that describes our culture: "Keep the main thing the main thing." It means that although learning more about our faith is an important life-long endeavor, everything we believe, think, say, and do is rooted in the gospel. It's a reminder to the brilliant to avoid drifting into academic elitism and a comfort to those young in their faith—that they are not unqualified just because they don't have all the answers.

Let's take a look at a couple of biblical characters who might appear, at first glance, to be unqualified to advance God's kingdom but were used in awesome ways.

First, the Samaritan woman at the well *(John 4:4-30, 39-42).* I'll let you read the story for yourself, but here's the point. This woman was an outcast sinner with screwed-up theology. No one wanted to be around her, and she was living in sin. But when Jesus spoke to her and revealed Himself to be the Messiah, she couldn't help but tell others. She ran back into town—to all the people who avoided her—and begged them to come meet this man named Jesus. Pay close attention to what happened.

> *Many of the Samaritans from that town believed in him because of the woman's testimony, "He told me everything I ever did." So when the Samaritans came to him, they urged him to stay with them, and he stayed two days. And because of his words many more became believers. They said to the*

> woman, *"We no longer believe just because of what you said; now we have heard for ourselves, and we know that this man really is the Savior of the world." (vv. 39-42)*

The Samaritan woman had only known Jesus for five minutes but was so overwhelmed and overjoyed that she overflowed into others. Maybe a good word to describe her would be *catalyst*. We might think she's completely unqualified to play a part in God's mission, but God didn't think so.

How about Peter and John, two blue-collar fishermen with less of a formal education than most middle schoolers? If anyone was unqualified, they were. But they didn't let that stop them. One day, after being arrested and questioned for preaching the gospel, they stood and proclaimed:

> *Salvation is found in no one else, for there is no other name under heaven given to men by which we must be saved. (Acts 4:12)*

Bold words from common fishermen without a degree, huh? But here's the cool part—the part that we can hold on to when the fear of inadequacy rears its ugly head in our lives. Look at the response to their boldness.

> *When [the priests, temple guard, and Sadducees] saw the courage of Peter and John and realized they were unschooled, ordinary men, they were astonished and they took note that these men had been with Jesus. (Acts 4:13)*

We are qualified to share the good news because of *whom* we know, not just *what* we know. The prerequisites of evangelism are surrender, a changed heart, and an ongoing relationship with Christ.

When we are focused like Paul, intimate with Jesus like Peter and John, and overjoyed like the Samaritan woman, God *will* use us. He is faithful to use the faithful, not just the clever, talented, well-read, or impressive. Don't let the things you haven't yet learned keep you from sharing how God has transformed your life.

FEAR OF OFFENDING

As I write this, it is 2024, and it seems like the world has never seen more social and cultural landmines scattered around. Everything is offensive to someone. Even trying to be *inoffensive* is offensive to certain people. And don't even get me started on how offensive religion is, right? The fear of offending—remaining silent to avoid hurting, irritating, or insulting others—is enough to keep most Christians quiet.

- What if I say something that makes them mad or hurts them?
- What if they think I'm judging them because of their lifestyle or choices?

We're actually going to *start* with our key truth here, then unpack it in Scripture. Here's the thing, Christian. The gospel *is* offensive. We can't get around that fact. Following Jesus requires admission of guilt, genuine repentance, and complete surrender. That's hard to hear. I don't know if I've encountered anyone who smiled the first time they heard the words, "You are a sinner."

However, despite being hard truth to hear, the gospel leads to great hope, joy, and peace. What is initially offensive turns out to be for our greatest good.

Let me use an example. I was in sixth grade the first time I realized I had body odor. Gross, I know. Only, I didn't realize it in the morning. I realized it at church on a Wednesday night surrounded by a bunch of other kids. If you've ever known an eleven-year-old boy, you know that he's not the most observant, so I'm not actually the one who first noticed my stench. My friend did. He pulled me aside and said, "Dude, you reek." I initially got mad at him for saying something so unkind, but then I took a whiff. . . and realized the most loving thing he could have done was tell me I stank.

The gospel may be offensive, but Scripture shows us that offensive things can be incredibly effective when done in love. I think of Peter's sermon from Acts 2:14-41. After being filled with the Holy Spirit, Peter stood up and began to preach the gospel. But instead of a nice, welcoming invitation for people to come to the front and accept Jesus as their personal Lord and Savior, he ended his sermon like this.

> *Therefore, let all Israel be assured of this: God has made this Jesus, whom you crucified, both Lord and Messiah. (Acts 2:31)*

Peter said, "You killed the Messiah!" And their response to this offensive truth was conviction. They said, "What shall we do?" and Peter told them to repent, receive the forgiveness of

Christ, and be filled with the Spirit themselves. He welcomed them into the family of God by being honest but loving.

Peter didn't revel in the "*Gotcha!*" statement. He wasn't being petty or mean. He was sharing the gospel in a way that would resonate with them and calling them to repent and surrender to God.

The gospel *is* offensive, but we don't need to be unduly offensive when sharing it. We share it boldly, but with patience, gentleness, and grace. We share it out of *real* love for others, not judgment. Remember, we were once far from God, too.

FEAR OF FAILURE

A massive gap for many people is the fear of failure—remaining silent to avoid making the situation worse.

- What if I let God down? He's going to be so disappointed in me.
- What if I ruin Jesus for someone by saying something wrong or not being clear enough?

We could blame our fast-paced, results-oriented, performance-driven culture for this one, but I think it goes deeper than that. I believe this root comes from a subtle misunderstanding we have about evangelism. In fact, we're going to dedicate an entire element to the idea of success and failure in God's mission, but for now, let's look at a parable taught by Jesus.

In Matthew 25:14-30, we find the parable of the talents. In this parable, a master left his three servants in charge of different amounts of money according to their ability. To one servant the master gave five talents (about 375 pounds of gold), to another, two talents, and to another, one. Rather than limiting this parable to the topic of money, look at it this way: God has placed you in a context. We talked about that in the last chapter. He has given you gifts, relationships, experiences, and a brand-new heart. What He has given *me* might look different than what He has given you. My wife is an introvert. She interacts with fewer people than I do, but here's the thing: God doesn't judge her by my standard or vice versa.

In this story, the servant who had five talents was faithful and made five more, and the master said, *"Well done, good and faithful servant!"* The one who was given two made two more, and the master said the same. But the servant who was given one talent panicked and buried his money. Finally, when the master approached him, this servant said, *"I was afraid and went out and hid your talent in the ground. See, here is what belongs to you."* But instead of responding with, "Well done!" the master called him a failure.

But look a little deeper. *Why* did the master say this servant failed? Because he never even tried. This is where we find our encouragement when faced with the fear of failure. God is in control, just like the master in the story. He has called us, equipped us, and sent us to *invest* ourselves into others. True failure is burying our gifts, experiences, context, and calling. I like to say that the easiest way to fail in evangelism is by keeping our mouths shut.

God has never required perfection, only faithfulness. He chose to change the world through imperfect people dependent upon Him. Short of sharing a blatantly false gospel (see Element One) any faithful attempt to share the hope of Jesus with someone who needs to hear it is a success. Again, more on this in the next chapter.

FEAR OF HYPOCRISY

The final fear of the bunch is a nasty one. It's nasty because it's true. The fear of hypocrisy—remaining silent due to personal failures, flaws, or disobedience—slithers into our minds and quietly destroys any hope of feeling qualified or worthy to join God's mission.

- They know I'm not perfect. What right do I have?
- What if they bring up my sins and claim they're no worse than I am?

So, why did I say it was true? I didn't say that about the other ones. Well, were you given a new heart, saved from eternal separation from God, and called to imitate Christ? Yeah, me too. Obviously you never sin anymore, right? Oh, you do? Yeah, me too. So, what does that make us? Hypocrites.

But here's the thing about Christian hypocrisy. God expects it. God *knows* you won't be perfect. He's not shocked when you fall down.

When my kids learned to walk, I celebrated every step. Not once did I stand across the room with my arms outstretched only to berate them when they fell over. One step—fall. Two steps—fall. Three steps, four steps—fall. Every single time, I picked them up, hugged them, and we tried again. And every time they *failed*, they were frustrated, sure, but they never felt shame, because they knew dad was there to pick them up, to hold their hand, to practice with them, and to be a guide as they figured out the mechanics.

Your relationship with God is alive, and it takes time to learn how to live His way. You have to work out spiritual muscles you didn't even know you had, but it's about growth—progress, not perfection. We may have already introduced this verse, but let's revisit it in this context, because—let's be honest—you may have already forgotten how this works. I know I often do...

> *If we claim to be without sin, we deceive ourselves and the truth is not in us. If we confess our sins, he is faithful and just and will forgive us our sins and purify us from all unrighteousness. If we claim we have not sinned, we make him out to be a liar and his word is not in us. My dear children, I write this to you so that you will not sin. But if anybody does sin, we have an advocate with the Father—Jesus Christ, the Righteous One. He is the atoning sacrifice for our sins, and not only for ours but also for the sins of the whole world. (1 John 1:8-2:2)*

You sin, remember? Don't pretend like you don't. But because of your new identity in Christ and what He did on the cross, you're invited to lay those sins at the feet of Jesus. He *promises* to forgive and He has the *right* to forgive. Don't sin... but when you do, remember that Jesus paid for it.

Fall forward. Fall into His arms. Lean into Christ when you fall, don't run and hide, because the beauty of the gospel is highlighted by our imperfection.

The difference between your sin and the sin of someone who doesn't know God is that yours doesn't separate you from Him anymore. So be honest. Own your mistakes. But don't let them keep you quiet, wallowing in guilt and shame. Much like David after his colossal failure with Bathsheba and her husband, Uriah *(2 Sam. 11-12)*, give praise to God and tell others of His great love.

> *Deliver me from the guilt of bloodshed, O God, you who are God my Savior, and my tongue will sing of your righteousness. Open my lips, Lord, and my mouth will declare your praise. (Psalm 51:14-15)*

LACK OF URGENCY

Our lack of urgency is, I believe, the most quietly pervasive gospel gap we experience. I say that because, unlike some of the others, we don't spend much time thinking about it; and when we do, it's easy to make excuses for this one. Definitionally, the lack of urgency is remaining silent due to a misunderstanding of God's mission.

- I don't have the time or energy right now. I'm sure I'll get to them eventually.
- Someone else will share the gospel with them. God is sovereign, after all.

I won't take extra time explaining this root, and I won't mince words. The lack of urgency comes from comfortable, apathetic faith—faith that says, "I got my salvation, and I'll get to you when and if I get a chance."

D.T. Niles, Sri Lankan pastor and theologian, described evangelism simply as one beggar telling another beggar where to get food.[8] Giving a hungry man a meal *should* cause him to empathize with all those who are still hungry. Similarly, experiencing salvation, adoption, purpose, and intimacy with God *should* propel us toward anyone still wandering in darkness. And yet, we're often content to find someplace to sit and enjoy our meal.

James captured this tendency in chapter 2 of his letter.

> *What good is it, my brothers and sisters, if someone claims to have faith but has no deeds? Can such faith save them? Suppose a brother or a sister is without clothes and daily food. If one of you says to them, "Go in peace; keep warm and well fed," but does nothing about their physical needs, what good is it? In the same way, faith by itself, if it is not accompanied by action, is dead. (James 2:14-17)*

Believe it or not, evangelism—the act of bringing the gospel to those who are suffering—*is* a deed. It's a work that we do, not only for the joy and new life of others, but our own joy! Being used by God is an amazing experience, and our obedience does not return void. A lack of urgency reveals more about our hearts than we realize. It reveals our immaturity and misunderstanding of what God truly desires from His children. But like many other things in this book, it is an indicator that we need to calibrate and open our eyes, not an indictment that we are unworthy or unloved.

---

8 D.T. Niles, *That They May Have Life* (New York: Harper & Brothers, 1951), 96

LACK OF LOVE

Our final root is the hardest to stomach. It's difficult because it reminds us of who we once were. The lack of love—remaining silent due to a personal grudge, opinion, or attitude—is a blindfold that strips us of Christ's eyes and causes us to see others through the lens of pain, entitlement, and anger.

- What if God actually changes someone I hate?
- That person doesn't deserve to be saved because of how he's hurt me.

We don't have to look much further than the story of Jonah to understand our human tendency to judge others. When I was a kid, I thought the book of Jonah was about a guy getting swallowed by a fish, but that's only one small detail. Here's the *whole* story. Jonah was a prophet instructed by God travel to a place called Nineveh and deliver a message: "Repent and turn to the Lord or you will be destroyed." Instead, he sailed in the opposite direction. When a huge storm showed up, Jonah knew it was because he ran from God, so he asked the crew to throw him overboard. Enter fish, stage left. Jonah was swallowed, vomited up on the shore of Ninevah, and ended up delivering God's message despite his initial disobedience. And wouldn't you know it. . . 120,000 Ninevites repented and turned to the Lord. God didn't have to destroy Ninevah after all!

Jonah was probably ecstatic, right? Well. . . Check out his reaction. Trust me, it's not pretty.

> *But to Jonah this seemed very wrong, and he became angry. He prayed to the L*ORD*, "Isn't this what I said, L*ORD*, when I was still at home? That is what I tried to forestall by fleeing to Tarshish. I knew that you are a gracious and compassionate God, slow to anger and abounding in love, a God who relents from sending calamity. Now, L*ORD*, take away my life, for it is better for me to die than to live." (Jonah 4:1-3)*

Jonah told God, "I *knew* you would save them. That's why I ran." He hated the Ninevites so much that he was furious when they repented and God relented.

I've been hurt before—attacked for no good reason. In these moments, I understand Jonah's anger. And just like so many of the other gaps, I begin to let it affect my role in God's mission. Suddenly, *I* am judge, jury, and executioner. I begin to see people as *too bad* or *unsavable* and refuse to even try. See? I told you it was rough.

So how do we combat a lack of love? We remember the one who, Himself, *is* love *(1 John 4:8).*

> *You see, at just the right time, when we were still powerless, Christ died for the ungodly. Very rarely will anyone die for a righteous person, though for a good person someone might possibly dare to die. But God demonstrates his own love for us in this: While we were still sinners, Christ died for us. (Rom. 5:6-8)*

While I was still an enemy of God, He died for me. He did it to demonstrate His great love. He didn't do it because I am worthy or because I played by the rules. He did it *despite* my behavior.

Let's not forget that the gospel has the power to change even the darkest of hearts. The antidote to hatred and judgment is to remember God's forgiveness and our transformation. It is the only way to love like Christ and overcome our lack of love.

PRACTICE PRACTICE PRACTICE

After discovering your unique gospel gaps, tracing them back to common roots, and holding them up to the truth of God's Word, it's important to bring them to life. After all, identifying gaps is only half the battle. Overcoming them is what builds real confidence.

I *love* playing pretend, whether it's Legos with my kids or evangelism practice. That's all practice is—a helpful game of pretend where the stakes don't matter. Instead of trying to learn how to overcome your gaps in real time—with people who don't know Jesus—grab a Christian friend and begin creating hypothetical worst-case scenarios to see how you might navigate conversations that elicit your gospel gaps. Recreate real situations that have gone poorly for you in the past—times you wish you would have gone a different direction or said something more clearly. Pretend to be different people and notice how each person triggers a different gap. Practice because people are worth our effort, and the gospel is worth our proficiency.

ANSWERS AND ANTIDOTES

Are you hesitant to share the gospel? Probably. But armed with an understanding of gospel gaps, ways to identify them, and key biblical truths, you can press through your hesitation because you know you're not alone. You have the antidote to fear—trust in an almighty God who has called you to rest in His power, not your own. So, when the enemy whispers a gap or two in your ear, remind him that our human hesitations and limitations are nothing to God, remember all the faithful brothers and sisters in Christ who faced the very same gaps, and boldly share the gospel.

ASK YOURSELF

- Have I ever thought specifically about why I don't share my faith with others?
- What are some of my biggest gospel gaps? When was the last time they stopped me from having a gospel conversation?
- How can Scripture help me overcome my gospel gaps?
- Have I ever practiced gospel conversations with safe people in a safe environment?

Element Six
THE ROLE

Am I confident in how God uses me?

FISH IN THE TREES

There's an old saying often attributed to Albert Einstein that says, "If you judge a fish by its ability to climb a tree, it will live its whole life believing that it is stupid." This illustration is meant to be as absurd as it sounds. Of course fish can't climb trees! They were never intended to climb trees, no one expects them to climb trees, and anyone judging them by that metric should probably spend some more time learning about fish. I hear they have great schools, by the way.

The point is that placing incorrect or unattainable expectations on people will do nothing but crush their spirit and alienate them. Oh, and you can kiss any shred of confidence goodbye.

Element Six—*The Role*—is incredibly important for anyone desiring to live an outward-focused life. Misunderstanding what God expects from us, trying to accomplish what only He can do, and measuring success incorrectly will snuff out even the most passionate evangelists.

So, what *is* our role in God's mission? What is God's role? Is it on our shoulders, or will He take care of it? And if He is in control, why should we even bother? Anyone with me?

It can be mind-boggling to try to follow all the threads of *how* God saves, so if you're looking for a deep dive into the theology and mechanics of salvation, I'm sorry to say you won't find it here. I'd like to talk, instead, about what we *do* know beyond a shadow of a doubt about our role and God's role in the salvation of others.

MINISTRY OF RECONCILIATION

I've said a few times that God invites us *into* His mission. He didn't simply hand it over to us. Paul describes it this way.

> *Therefore, if anyone is in Christ, the new creation has come: The old has gone, the new is here! All this is from God, who reconciled us to himself through Christ and gave us the ministry of reconciliation: that God was reconciling the world to himself in Christ, not counting people's sins against them. And he has committed to us the message of reconciliation. We are therefore Christ's*

ambassadors, as though God were making his appeal through us. We implore you on Christ's behalf: Be reconciled to God. God made him who had no sin to be sin for us, so that in him we might become the righteousness of God. (2 Cor. 5:17-21)

We were saved and made new. God reconciled us to Himself. He made us whole again, restoring our relationship with Him that was broken because of sin. But that's not all. He gave us something called the *ministry of reconciliation.* Wait. God gave us a ministry? If your pastor called you and said, "I'm giving you the youth ministry," what would that mean to you? Probably that you need brush up on your *Minute to Win It* games because you just got a new job, champ.

In this passage, we begin to see the nuance of our role in God's mission. He does the reconciling, but we act as agents of His: minsters of reconciliation and ambassadors of Christ. He equips us with the *message* of reconciliation: the gospel—that He took our sin and gave us His righteousness. Nowhere in this passage can we make the claim that we are in charge; we simply play a role. And that role is a gift.

My son wants nothing more than to help me with projects around the house. He has his own tools, work clothes, and a little headlamp to help me see into dark places. This little copy of mine, made in my image, finds so much joy in helping his dad, but he would never tell you he's in charge. He is overwhelmingly confident in his role as my *helper* because he doesn't feel the weight of the whole project on his shoulders.

Evangelism is just the same. We are invited into God's

project—the redemption of the lost—and when we understand our role, nothing could possibly bring us more joy. So, let's get specific. We're helpers, agents, ambassadors, and reconcilers. But what do we practically *do* in God's mission? I like to use this little graphic to help me wrap my mind around it.

REALIZING OUR ROLE

Much like our discussion about motivation, we need to consider the parties involved in this process: God, us, and them. Who does what? Let's start with us. I believe there are three actions we can take on a daily basis.

The *first* is prayer. We are called to pray for God to change the hearts of those far from Him as Paul does in Romans

10:1 when he prays for the Israelites to be saved.

And because we are His children, in a loving relationship with Him, we have unhindered access to approach Him whenever we want *(Heb. 4:14-16)*. The fancy term for it is *intercessory prayer* or praying on behalf of others.

The *second* action we can take is something we'll unpack more in the following chapter—sharing the gospel. Don't forget that we've been building something—an outward-focused worldview that causes our faith to overflow into those around us. When we spend time cultivating the eight elements found in this book, evangelism *will* become more natural. However, we can't rely completely on natural, organic evangelism. Gaps will arise and we'll need to respond with obedience to faithfully share the gospel with *anyone* who needs it, regardless of the spiritual potential we see in that person.

What else could we possibly *do* in this process? Well, I think this *third* action is often overlooked. And when it *is* talked about, it's done from a *passive* point of view. But trust me, there is nothing passive about this one. We trust. If you've ever experienced a trust fall—falling blindly into the outstretched arms of others—you know that trust is not a passive trait, but an active choice. "Will they catch me?" "What if they don't?" Trust doesn't come naturally. It is a learned skill. We *place* our trust in God like my son places his trust in me, believing that I know the plan as we put together a chicken coop or hang a ceiling fan. Our trust is so important because we can't see the whole picture. We don't know what God is doing behind the scenes and how He's working in the hearts of the lost.

> *Trust in the* L<small>ORD</small> *with all your heart and lean not on your own understanding; in all your ways submit to him, and he will make your paths straight. (Prov. 3:5-6)*

So, what's our role? We hit our knees every day, praying for God to do what only He can do. We move, taking steps to share good news with those who need it. And we trust, resting in God's sovereignty and His ability to bring dead things to life.

When we realize our role, God's role becomes abundantly clear. It's everything else. God changes hearts—we don't. And He does it according to His plan, purpose, and timing. He is faithful to call the lost, drawing them to Himself and welcoming them into His family just like He did for you and me.

THE AGRICULTURE OF EVANGELISM

Understanding our role removes the pressure we often feel to trick, convince, scare, or bribe people into a profession of faith just so we can feel accomplished. I remember a conversation I had with a young man when I was in college. A misunderstanding of my role caused me to bombard this poor kid with every method, trick, and scare tactic I could think of, only to walk away feeling like a failure because he didn't decide to follow Jesus. To be clear, I was upset because, as a fish, I couldn't climb a tree.

The things we *do* aren't the only important pieces of this puzzle. We must also measure success correctly. What does it mean to *succeed* in evangelism? If it isn't closing the deal, what is it? Let's take a look at what Scripture has to say.

In 1 Corinthians, Paul wrote to address divisions happening in the church. Christians were essentially choosing sides, some claiming to follow Paul and others claiming to follow a talented teacher named Apollos. And although Paul wasn't *specifically* writing about evangelism, his words resonate loudly in the minds of those wrestling with their role.

> *What, after all, is Apollos? And what is Paul? Only servants, through whom you came to believe—as the Lord has assigned to each his task. I planted the seed, Apollos watered it, but God has been making it grow. So neither the one who plants nor the one who waters is anything, but only God, who makes things grow. The one who plants and the one who waters have one purpose, and they will each be rewarded according to their own labor. (1 Cor. 3:5-8)*

Paul used the example of agriculture to explain the process of spiritual growth. Let's bring his example to life. My wife likes to garden. She carefully tills the soil and lovingly plants the seeds, but often forgets to water them. So, as I walk by the garden and see the fledgling plants wilting, I give them a quick shower with the hose. Our kids, however, are the ones who are first to notice the ripe strawberries, so they pick them and bring them inside for the family to enjoy. Now you tell me: who is responsible for the delicious bowl of fruit in our kitchen?

Our confidence doesn't come from our ability, but from our faithfulness and trust in God's ability. Sometimes you'll plant—getting the opportunity to share the hope of Jesus with someone for the very first time. Other times, you'll water—reminding someone of His goodness even though that person has heard it before. And sometimes, through no special talent of your own, you'll get to harvest—praying with someone ready to begin a life with Christ.

The key here is to think about all that God is doing in the hearts and minds of others. He is weaving a tapestry of faith in the lives of those around us. We may not be able to see the whole picture, but are we willing to be a thread—to plant, knowing that someone else might get the joy of harvesting? Will we water again and again, not knowing if we'll ever see the finished product?

In 2009, my older sister moved to an extremely challenging part of Africa to work among Muslims. She and her husband spent a decade ministering to anyone who would listen, living their lives on mission, and faithfully sharing the good news. But by the time they left, ten long years later, they had seen little, if any, spiritual fruit. No radical transformation stories. No revival.

I asked my sister one day about that time. Specifically, "How did you do it? Didn't you feel like a failure?" Her response took my breath away. She told me that they simply spent ten years planting and watering, resting in God's timing, not their own. So, no. She didn't feel like a failure. Just a part of God's plan.

Jesus captured this idea as He taught His disciples about sowing and reaping a spiritual harvest.

> *Thus the saying "One sows and another reaps" is true. I*

THE ROLE

sent you to reap what you have not worked for. Others have done the hard work, and you have reaped the benefits of their labor. (John 4:37-38)

I can only imagine the scene as a new missionary family lands in that same African country one day. I wish I was a fly on the wall as people who heard the gospel from my sister and brother-in-law in 2013 hear it again years later and hit their knees in surrender.

Success in evangelism isn't measured by immediate *conversions*, but by faithful *conversations* about the gospel. Yes, our ultimate goal is the salvation of others, but when we understand our role and God's role, we can trust in His plan, purpose, and timing.

OUTWARD-FOCUSED PRAYER

Before we move on to the next element, let's talk a bit more about prayer. Just like sharing the gospel and trusting God's plan and timing, outward-focused prayer keeps us focused both upward—toward God, and outward—toward those we want to reach.

Developing an outward-focused prayer life is a process not unlike our own human growth and development. Like children, we begin by asking our Father to *help* us. In the early days of our faith, we're mainly concerned with our own struggles, worries, and needs, and He lovingly answers. As we mature, we begin to notice the needs of others and ask our Father to *help* them, too.

A little later, we see our need to be *changed*. We understand our sinful tendencies and ask for God's help to change our hearts, minds, and actions. This, too, grows to include others as we desire for *them* to live as God intended for their good and His glory.

Finally, after developing healthy habits of asking for God's help and regularly calibrating to His will, we ask Him to *use* us. Much like a twenty-one-year-old ready to join the family business, we understand our role in God's mission and are eager to begin. Further maturity reveals how God uses *all* believers, not just us, and we begin to pray for others to be used as well.

These stages are all crucial to an outward-focused prayer life. It's important to remember that earlier stages don't disappear as we grow. Each one—help, change, and use—plays an important role in a life on mission. For example, a mature believer prays that God would use him to reach others, but still calls out for His help in difficult situations and asks to be made more like Christ every day.

The function of prayer is not the only thing that expands as we mature. Our *focus* does, too. We move from praying *reactively* to *proactively*.

Reactive prayer focuses on past or present situations. Scripture tells us to present our requests to God to receive His unexplainable peace *(Phil. 4:4-7)*. He is pleased to hear from us about our struggles and circumstances. But there's another aspect to prayer that I think we often miss—proactive prayer: what God *can* and *will* do in the future or in places we can't go. This is likely the most underutilized weapon we have in our evangelistic arsenal, and it's only possible when we view our role rightly. So, now that we've done that, let's lock and load.

James reminds us that when we're intimate with God, our prayers are powerful and effective *(James 5:16b)*, and Psalm 34:15 claims that the Lord is attentive to the cries of the righteous. In Luke 18, Jesus tells His disciples a parable to remind them to keep praying and never give up.

Put it together. As we abide in Christ, He is attentive to our prayers—powerful prayers that matter in the grand scheme of things. So, we don't give up. We keep bringing our requests to God, asking Him to work in and through others as only He can. Beautiful, isn't it? One last example: Paul concludes his letter to the Ephesian church this way.

> *And pray in the Spirit on all occasions with all kinds of prayers and requests. With this in mind, be alert and always keep on praying for all the Lord's people. Pray also for me, that whenever I speak, words may be given me so that I will fearlessly make known the mystery of the gospel, for which I am an ambassador in chains. Pray that I may declare it fearlessly, as I should. (Eph. 6:18-20)*

As we understand the function and focus of evangelistic prayer, let's not forget frequency. There's no better verse than 1 Thessalonians 5:17 to remind us how often God wants to hear from us. It says we are to *"pray without ceasing."* Those words are not a burden, but an invitation to approach God at any time.

Ask yourself: "How much time do I spend talking to God each day?" and "How much time do I spend praying for *others* each day?" Once we wrestle with questions like these, we can begin to introduce new prayer habits that keep our eyes fixed on Jesus and our hearts focused outward.

THE BIG PICTURE

Understanding the role we play in God's mission takes time, but as each thread in the tapestry falls into place, a breathtaking picture is revealed. We catch a glimpse of what God is doing and find joy, purpose, and belonging as we join Him. I have watched this element transform lives. I've watched it free Christians from the chains of accomplishment, and I've seen a lot of fish who've spent years feeling stupid, suddenly realize how important it is to swim.

ASK YOURSELF

- What are some common misconceptions about the role of Christians in evangelism? How could misunderstanding my role impact my faith?
- What role does prayer play? How have I seen God change people through prayer?
- How can my prayer life become more outward-focused?

Element Seven
THE PLAN

Is my preparation fueled by love?

DISCIPLESHIP IN THE DETAILS

Living an outward-focused life doesn't happen by accident any more than throwing a touchdown pass in the Superbowl. It takes dedication, practice, vulnerability, and, yes, preparation.

"But Andrew," you might be asking, "didn't you say we shouldn't focus on *closing the deal* or coming up with some formula to make sure people pray a salvation prayer? You said we're supposed to trust God and His plan." I absolutely did say that, but just because we're going to talk about preparation doesn't mean we forget everything we've already learned. Actually, it's only *because* of what we've discussed that we're ready to tackle what it looks like to make plans.

Strategy and planning are not dirty words in evangelism. They're only harmful when we separate them from Christ. Element Seven makes an enormous assumption right off the bat. Did you catch it? Whereas other elements asked simple *yes* or *no* questions, *The Plan* asks a very pointed, leading question—*Is my preparation fueled by love?* What's the assumption? That we're preparing!

I often get the opportunity to preach at various churches, camps, and retreats. When I accept the responsibility to deliver God's Word, I enter into a supernatural process. Like we just discussed in Element Six, I play a small role in what God is doing that Sunday morning in the hearts and minds of all who hear the message. The salvation of each congregant does not rest on my ability to preach a good sermon, and yet I spend hours preparing—carefully studying Scripture, thinking of personal examples that will make the text explode with color in the lives of each person, and discerning how to approach each church uniquely based on its denominational and congregational identity.

In short, I *prepare* rigorously for a work that doesn't rest solely on me. Does reading commentaries mean I don't trust God's Spirit to lead and guide me? Absolutely not. Does considering the average age and surrounding community of each group mean I'm being devious in my delivery? No. I put in the hard work to prepare because I want to represent God and Scripture well, I want to make sure my message comes across clearly, and I want each person to feel cared for. I plan because I love.

One of my mantras, of which there are many, is "Planning matters because people matter." My goal is not to trick people, but to impact them in the most appropriate, effective way I can. I want to see others as people, not projects—as individuals with unique stories, not as salvation statistics. Much like sermon preparation, we are called to prepare before participating in God's supernatural work. We do this by asking good questions, praying specific things, and practicing different scenarios. Why? Because people are worth it to Jesus, so people should be worth it to us.

GREATEST GOSPEL NEED

Speaking of Jesus, He had an uncanny ability to identify what I like to call *points of greatest gospel need*—unique areas of each person's life in desperate need of hope, forgiveness, or redemption. He saw people as unique individuals, called out something He noticed, then connected that thing to a truth about God and His kingdom.

I often reference the story of the rich young ruler when explaining this idea. We don't know his name, yet he appears in Matthew, Mark, and Luke. What we *do* know from those accounts is that this man had money, he had his whole life ahead of him, and he had status—he was important. I find it fascinating how quickly Jesus located this man's point of greatest gospel need. The young man asked Jesus, "What must I do to inherit eternal life?" and after repeating the Great Commandment to love God and love others, Jesus hit the bullseye.

> *You still lack one thing. Sell everything you have and give to the poor, and you will have treasure in heaven. Then come, follow me. (Luke 18:22)*

Jesus essentially said, "Give me your wealth—your money and possessions. Give me your future—your aspirations and plans. And give me your status—we're leaving this place and no one will know who you are once we do." But instead of responding in surrender and joy, the young man walked away sad because of his great wealth. We don't know what happened to this man—whether he eventually realized his need for a Savior or remained smothered by his possessions and popularity, but Jesus knew him and exactly how he needed to hear the good news. Jesus identified his point of greatest gospel need and tailored His call to fit it.

There are many examples of Jesus doing this—acknowledging individuals and identifying *how* they needed to hear the good news, not just *that* they needed it.

PRAYING ON PURPOSE

It doesn't take much to identify the specific needs of those around us. We just have to be willing to put in the work—to prepare. There are two ways I encourage people to prepare: intentional prayer and introspective questions.

Everyone would benefit from the blanket prayer, "Dear God, please prepare _____'s heart to receive the gospel." But I believe it's important to think a little more deeply about the people we want to reach.

First, ask yourself, "*Who* am I praying for?" Who is this person? What's his or her story? Maybe you identified some *neighbors* you want to impact with the gospel all the way back in chapter four when we talked about *The Lost*.

Next, based on what you know about them, ask yourself, "*What* am I praying for?" What do you want to see God do in each person's life? Specifically.

Finally, "*Why* am I praying these things for these people?" Why do these specific prayer points stand out? What could God do in their lives through your prayers?

Although they look similar, each question challenges us in a unique way. Answering *"what"* draws our minds to the spiritual state of others and the specific things preventing them from following Christ, while answering *"why"* challenges us to consider each neighbor as a unique individual.

Be as specific and detailed as possible in your prayers. The goal is to consider each person's story and what you'd like to see God do in his or her life. When we pray on purpose, everyone wins. We are drawn *toward the lost* as we lift their unique stories up to the Lord, and *toward God* as we rely on His plan and timing. Those far from Christ are drawn *toward God* as we pray, and *toward us* as we lovingly pursue them.

PRACTICAL PRAYER HABITS

Praying intentionally for others might be a new habit for you. Sure, it might be a little awkward at first, but it's an incredibly effective way to humanize the people we love and care for them on a deep and personal level. Here are a few practical tips as you start this journey of praying on purpose.

- Consider each person daily, taking time to pray for them one by one.
- Don't overcommit! If you're not used to praying for a long time, it's unrealistic to think you can start that habit in one day.
- Start small. Dedicate a couple minutes to each person at first, extending the time as you grow.
- Write down details and add them to your prayer list as new things come to mind or your relationship deepens.
- Let your prayers be fueled by love and care for others, not obligation.

CONSIDERING CONVERSATIONS

The second way to identify points of greatest gospel need is to ask good introspective questions. After spending some time praying for someone, ask yourself, "Has anything stood out to me during prayer?" God is good and often impresses things on our minds and hearts that we wouldn't see if we weren't abiding in Him and seeking His will above our own.

Ask, "Have I shown genuine interest in this person's life recently?" Imagine how unnatural it would seem if someone approached you to learn about your spiritual background and opinions and then ignored you, only to return and present the gospel. Take the time to think about your relationships with others and whether each individual feels loved by you or like a project.

Here's another good one. Ask, "Are there any important details I should remember about this person before I share the gospel?" Is she gay? Muslim? Struggling with church hurt? Do you know? And how does this information help to reveal her point of greatest gospel need and direct you to appropriate ways to share the gospel? What barriers has she constructed to keep God out, and what's the most loving way to navigate those barriers. See what a good question can reveal? Let's care enough to know enough.

One more. Obviously we want to see people come to saving faith in Jesus, but maybe before starting a conversation, take the time to ask, "What specifically am I trying to accomplish with *this* person in *this* conversation?" Sometimes all we're trying to do is introduce someone to God's love. Other times, we just want to answer questions about faith. Considering specific conversation goals can help us focus on one thing at a time instead of feeling the need to blast people with information. It also helps us prepare more effectively. If my goal is to let a friend know how good Jesus is and to share my testimony, I can spend time thinking and praying about those things before I open my mouth.

When we pray intentionally, ask good, introspective questions, and consider each person's point of greatest gospel need, God will reveal the best method and timing for us to follow through and share the good news.

MIXING UP THE METHOD

Think back with me all the way to Element One—*The Gospel*. I claimed, so many pages ago, that the same message can (and should) be shared in many different ways. Does it make sense now? We don't use different methods to be cute or clever. We put in the work to learn them and discern when to use them so when people—real people—cross our path, we can most effectively inject hope into their point of greatest gospel need.

Would you use the Romans Road method with someone who denies the truth of Scripture? Probably not. Instead, you might point to the brokenness all around us and ask that person why *he* thinks the world is fractured. Should we introduce the idea of God as our Father to someone who has been mistreated, abandoned, or abused by her earthly father? Maybe yes, maybe no. Depending on the details of her story and the leading of the Spirit of God, the best thing you could do might be to highlight a perfect, heavenly Father. Or it could be the worst thing, jamming a huge wedge into the conversation, and potentially your relationship.

Do you see why we don't just memorize methods? Planning matters because people matter. *Both* parts of that statement are important. We should get to know everything we possibly can about people, and we should prepare vigorously to bring them the gospel, but it must all be fueled by love or we'll simply be an annoying gong or clanging cymbal *(1 Cor. 13:1)*.

TIME TO GO

I said it before and I'll say it again for the people in the back. People are worth our planning and practice. Think of the time you've spent reading this book. You're planning. You're practicing. You're thinking outside your own little world and taking steps to live an outward-focused life. It's amazing how simple it all seems once we put it together. Every part is important. Knowing the gospel, checking the heart, living lives that glorify God, seeking the lost, filling gaps, realizing the role we play, and planning with love all lead us to this moment. It's critically important to plan, but at some point it's time to *go*.

Our next chapter will deal with reactions and next steps—what comes *after* we have bold gospel conversations. So, take a moment to soak it in. You're ready. You've been given the tools—the *elements*—necessary to share the gospel. But for those who still don't feel quite ready, let's walk through one more exercise together.

Gospel conversations should exist somewhere between calculated and convenient. We should be intentional, but not aggressive or forceful. On the other hand, we shouldn't just wait for the picture-perfect moment to present itself. Trust me; it probably won't. Disciple making is uncomfortable, but it's important to identify *why* we feel uncomfortable before jumping into conversations. So, if you're one of the people who, despite making it this far, don't feel *ready*, ask yourself the following three questions.

- Have I been praying consistently for the person I want to reach?
- Do I feel spiritually full—connected to Christ?
- Have I identified and surrendered my gaps with the person I'm hesitant to approach?

If you answered *yes* to these three questions, push through the discomfort. Your hesitation is coming from the enemy who is prowling around like a roaring lion, trying to devour you *(1 Peter 5:8)*, to kill, steal, and destroy you *(John 10:10a)*, or at the very least, to keep you quiet.

If you answered *no* to any one of these three questions, stop and focus on addressing the issue before moving on. Remember? Somewhere between calculated and convenient. We don't pause and calibrate out of apathy, but urgency. And yet, we recognize that charging forward unprepared and ill-equipped is dangerous not only to others but also to us. Begin praying, lean into Christ, and spend some time contemplating and practicing solutions for your gaps, then step forward in faith.

FORTUNE FAVORS THE BOLD

When we faithfully prepare to share the gospel, we grow in confidence and boldness. Preparation and planning protect us from seeing evangelism as a spur-of-the-moment activity. Without them, the fear of messing up or coming across unprepared can paralyze us. God has a habit of advancing His kingdom through broken but bold people—people who love Him and love others; people who are willing to put their reputations, futures, and very lives on the line so others might know Christ; people who remember the very first and very last words of the Great Commission—the comfort surrounding the command.

All authority in heaven and on earth has been given to me.

Therefore go and make disciples of all nations, baptizing them in the name of the Father and of the Son and of the Holy Spirit, and teaching them to obey everything I have commanded you.

And surely I am with you always, to the very end of the age. (Matt. 28:18b-20)

The question we must ask ourselves is, "What am I waiting for?" God is at work in the lives of those around us. Let's love them enough to go and make disciples.

ASK YOURSELF

- How do preparation and planning help to effectively reach the lost? What if that preparation isn't fueled by love?
- Why is it helpful to remember details about the people I hope to reach?
- How could someone's context change the way I present the gospel?
- What are some of the most important things to remember before approaching others?

Element Eight
THE WIN

Am I celebrating every gospel conversation?

WHAT IF

I'm not what you would call a *dog-lover*. It's a fact that doesn't make me very popular. And before you do what everyone else does, and think, "If you only knew *my* dog, you'd change your mind." No. I promise I won't. I'm sure your dog is awesome, but I'm just not interested in getting acquainted.

Now, I'm not just a cold-hearted monster. I have trauma. When I was six years old, I accidentally spooked my friend's dog. And as I ran away, trying to remove myself from the situation, I was rewarded with a not-so-gentle bite. . . right on the hindquarters. See? Trauma. Sure, it happened over twenty-five years ago, but ever since then I have just had a distaste for dogs. As irrational as it sounds, every time I'm around a dog I wonder, "Is this dog going to bite me, too?"

This might feel like a strange way to begin a chapter, but I'm reminded of this experience every time people tell me about the negative reactions they received after sharing their faith. Being belittled, yelled at, or simply ignored for stepping out in boldness, much like getting chewed on by a dog, creates trauma. And if we're not careful, we can let that trauma color our opinion of, and participation in, God's mission. I've listened to many Christians relive stories about awkward or tense faith conversations, claiming they'll never try again because it went so poorly.

This last chapter is dedicated to Element Eight—*The Win*. How can we leave any and every gospel conversation celebrating, no matter how people respond, and how can holding on to little wins ignite a fire in us to get back in the game when we feel like quitting?

RECEIVING REACTIONS

Let's start by discussing reactions. Every gospel conversation will be met with one of three reactions: positive, neutral, or negative. That's it. Only three. However, much like the dialects and roots from Element Five, these reactions might present themselves in a number of unique ways.

A positive reaction to the gospel might look like someone

giving his life to Christ for the very first time. It doesn't get much more positive than that, does it? Or maybe you'll go on to share the gospel with someone who gave her life to Christ in the past but has drifted or walked away from Him. The gospel isn't just for nonbelievers, you know. Christians need the gospel every day. One might even say we should be *rooted* in the gospel. Watching someone recommit her life to Christ after remembering her first love is a powerful experience and an overwhelmingly positive reaction.

How about something more subtle? A thoughtful, "Hmm" and a request to hear more is a way bigger deal than we sometimes realize. God can do wonders with curiosity. I think of all the people who have made the mistake of asking about my favorite football team. Buckle up, buttercup, because even though you didn't ask to become a card-carrying Miami Dolphins fan, I'm so glad you were curious! Positive.

Another positive reaction that's often overlooked is the acceptance of a church invitation or simply a second conversation. It might feel like a baby step, but we all started somewhere, didn't we? Just because your neighbor doesn't hit his knees and raise his hands doesn't mean God isn't working.

When I think about positive reactions, I often remember Nicodemus, the curious Pharisee who came to Jesus at night because he was afraid of what his peers might think. He had an incredible conversation with Jesus in which Jesus introduced him to the gospel—most notably, the famous John 3:16!

> *For God so loved the world that he gave his one and only Son, that whoever believes in him shall not perish but have eternal life.*

But Nicodemus didn't repent. . . not in that moment. We find him again in John 7, standing up to his fellow Pharisees on Jesus' behalf, and again at the tomb, honoring Jesus by wrapping His crucified body in expensive perfumes *(John 19:38-40)*. It may have taken multiple years and repeated encounters with Jesus, but Nicodemus' curiosity led him to eventual salvation and allegiance to Christ.

The second type of reaction is a neutral one. Neutral reactions are probably the most common, but that doesn't make them any easier to receive. There are many, many people walking around mistakenly believing that they are Christians. Some claim to be part of God's family because their parents are, they grew up in a Christian home, they go to church on Easter and Christmas, or think, "I'm a pretty good person."

You and I know that the only way to be saved is repentance of our sins and complete surrender to Christ *(John 14:6)*, and you realize that the people you're trying to reach with the gospel don't understand that, but they are adamant that they're already Christians. It's not a negative reaction, but it sure isn't positive. It's neutral—somewhere in between.

While I was a youth pastor, I routinely heard the phrase "I'll probably give my life to Christ when I'm older, just not right now. I want to have some fun as a kid first." Despite my internal screaming, I took it in stride, seeing it for what it was. Not a rejection, but not ideal. Neutral.

People may be confused by the gospel or misunderstand what you're trying to say. Others know what you're saying—they just don't really care. Overall, neutral reactions to the gospel are frustrating but manageable. They are not often the reason believers quit trying, just an uncomfortable bump in the road.

Speaking of quitting, let's talk about negative reactions. These are the scary ones—the worst-case scenarios we lie awake thinking about years later—like a dog bite. Someone who reacts negatively might become offended or angry, responding with a raised voice or retaliating with hurtful comments. Such a person might get defensive and bring up your shortcomings to try and gain the upper hand after being called a sinner. Many people are sarcastic and rude. You might be mocked or ridiculed for your faith. I know it's a bummer, but we need to talk about it.

In other cases, people might not be openly hostile; they'll just get awkward and avoid you, content to let the relationship fizzle out because you're just too *different*.

Finally, you might receive a polite, but firm, rejection that indicates clear disinterest, but a willingness to continue the relationship.

Negative reactions cause trauma. They stay with us for years, reminding us how we felt in the moment and promising us safety, belonging, and comfort in exchange for our silence.

I never said it would be easy, did I? Only that it's possible. I believe the main reason most Christians have taken themselves out of the gospel game is because they tried it once and didn't like how it ended up. But instead of being discipled after neutral or negative reactions, they were overcome by feelings of *failure*—"I've let God down," *rejection*—"No one will ever listen to me," *doubt*—"Maybe I did it wrong," or *awkwardness*—"Well, that relationship is over now..." Left unchecked, these feelings can have a profound effect on our intimacy with God and cause us to avoid gospel opportunities in the future.

But what's the title of this chapter again? Oh yeah, *The Win*. Stop being such a bummer, Andrew. I wholeheartedly believe that we can and should celebrate any reaction to the gospel: positive, neutral, and yes, even negative.

SUCCESS REVISITED

Being *prepared* to receive reactions is key to remaining confident and motivated. It can be tempting to abandon ship when people respond negatively or neutrally, but when we cling to God's truth about our role in the evangelistic process, we can remain steadfast and excited.

How did we define success earlier? *Faithful conversations, not immediate conversions.* When we remember this, neutral and negative reactions can be seen as planting and watering rather than failing. Did someone claim to be a Christian based on church attendance? Well, looking through God's missional lens, we can see that neutral reaction as an opportunity to water.

Look at it this way: if someone claims to be a Christian, even if his metric is off base, you can treat him like a brother in Christ. Suggest reading Scripture together, invite him to church, ask him to pray for you, and talk openly about the gospel. The metric will sort itself out as he either welcomes and enjoys spiritual things or realizes there might be more to faith than having Christian parents.

A negative reaction makes a lot of sense when you realize you just planted a seed of truth that goes against everything the world is trying to sell someone. What did you expect? Did you get a sarcastic and hurtful response? Well, I'm sometimes sarcastic when things hit a little too close to home, and I'm a Christian!

Seeing the big picture and celebrating *faithfulness*, not just positive reactions, helps us view seemingly fruitless conversations as *progress*. I can't imagine calling Jesus a failure, yet He was rejected by His own brothers *(John 7:5)* and abandoned by many of His followers *(John 6:66)*.

Need a more fallible example? Consider Stephen, the first martyr of the fledgling church. He was faithful to preach the gospel, and this was the reaction of the crowd.

> *When the members of the Sanhedrin heard this, they were furious and gnashed their teeth at him. But Stephen, full of the Holy Spirit, looked up to heaven and saw the glory of God, and Jesus standing at the right hand of God. "Look," he said, "I see heaven open and the Son of Man standing at the right hand of God." At this they covered their ears and, yelling at the top of their voices, they all rushed at him, dragged him out of the city and began to stone him. Meanwhile, the witnesses laid their coats at the feet of a young man named Saul. (Acts 7:54-58)*

Stephen's faithfulness led to his death, but it also planted (or watered) the seed that would lead to the salvation of a Christian-hunter named Saul, also known as Paul the apostle, author of the majority of our New Testament books. Stephen knew how to measure success. Do we? He knew how to celebrate when his circumstances were unimaginably dark and people charged at him with murderous intent. Do we? His eyes were fixed on *faithfulness* to the author and perfector of our faith *(Heb. 12:2)*, not just results. Are ours?

NAVIGATING NEXT STEPS

Regardless of the reaction, everyone who hears the gospel has a next step. This is the part of evangelistic training that is often left out. What happens *after* the gospel is presented? We should never give up on someone because of a neutral or negative reaction or simply hand that person off after a positive one. Part of living an outward-focused life is continually asking, "What's next?" Let's explore some potential next steps for each reaction.

If people react positively, consider praying *for* them and *with* them. You might even teach them what prayer is and how to do it if they're brand new to faith. You could plug them into your church or a solid local church in their area. Offer them accountability as they take their first steps of Christian living—being there for them as they fall and need a reminder to run toward God with their sin, not hide in shame. Connecting them with a mentor is another great idea. It could be someone who mentors you, someone looking for mentees, or even you! Send them encouraging verses and biblical truths. Maybe even start a Bible reading plan together. Sit with them and answer their questions. As I've said, curiosity is a beautiful thing, and we should never expect people to know everything right away.

What if they react neutrally? Well, you can still pray for them, can't you? If they haven't shut you down, you can insert your faith into everyday conversations, offer to answer any of their questions, or maybe even invite them to come to church with you on a Sunday that *isn't* Easter or Christmas. Follow up with them, check in, and revisit the gospel often. Send them worship songs, powerful sermons, helpful articles, or interesting Christian podcasts.

I like to think of it this way. I'm going to ask you a question, and you need to know before I ask it that there is a *right* answer and an *honest* answer to this question. Here it is. What do you do when you approach a yellow light while driving? All my right-answer people said, "Slow down." Good for you! It's the law, after all. But where are my honest people? You likely said, "Speed up! It's not red yet!" Neutral reactions are like yellow lights. I use this example half-jokingly, knowing that it breaks down if you take it too far, but my point remains. Until the neutral reaction turns negative, we can, and should, pursue people with love and discernment.

Finally, the negative reactions. There can't possibly be any next steps after someone yells at us, can there? Well, how would it look if you shared what you believe is the most important information imaginable with someone, only to turn tail and walk away when you didn't get what you wanted? Feels kind of icky, doesn't it? In fact, many cynics and people far from Christ are waiting for this very scenario to claim that Christians don't really love them and that they just want to score salvation points.

So, let's talk about some possible next steps after negative reactions. We can still pray for such people, can't we? We've talked at length about how important prayer can be, even when we're not present. What message would it send if someone viciously rejected you and you responded with unconditional love, diving even deeper into your friendship? That's not just the gospel message, but the life that should go with it. You can boldly maintain your Christian lifestyle around those who respond negatively. I don't know if you know this, but you *get* to be a Chrisitan. In fact, most people are okay with us believing whatever we want as long as we don't require them to believe it. So, be an unapologetic Christ-follower!

Offer to clarify their concerns or answer any questions. If you don't know the answer to something, just say the three magic words. "I. Don't. Know." It's okay not to know everything. Tell them you'll find out and get back to them. And finally, support them in tough times. My non-Christian friends may not follow Christ, but they often ask me to pray when things get tough because they know I have a relationship with God and that I would love nothing more than to pray *with* them and *for* them.

KNOW YOUR RESOURCES

When we share the gospel, we become spiritually responsible for those who hear it. Don't worry, that responsibility can look drastically different, depending on the people involved. For instance, when I share the gospel with my kids, I assume the responsibility to continue discipling them. They live with me! Contrast that to the man sitting next to me on a connecting flight to North Dakota. I will likely never see him again, but I still have a responsibility to do what I can in the time that I have.

In addition to knowing appropriate next steps for each reaction, it's important to know your *resources*. I may not be able to disciple everyone I reach with the gospel, but I can point anyone in the right direction.

The first resource I suggest is simple—God's Word. If she has a Bible, great! Where should she start reading it? Genesis? Revelation is popular these days. What if you were to suggest a book like Luke or John and explain to her that knowing *who* Jesus is makes the rest of the Bible come alive? That doesn't take much time or effort, does it? You could even help her find a good Bible app on her phone.

Next, think about other books and resources that have helped you grow in your faith. I regularly suggest the books *Radical* by David Platt and *Crazy Love* by Francis Chan. Why? Because when I was trying to figure out my faith, those were the books I read. If you only have a few moments, ask for his address, and offer to send him a copy or merely suggest he pursues some helpful materials on his own.

There's nothing quite like a good local church. The truth, community, and opportunity to serve in a body of Christ is critically important as we grow. Do you know the churches in your area? Would you be comfortable helping a new or potential believer find the right church family, even if it isn't yours?

Knowing the many ways God equips His people allows us to jump at spiritual responsibility, not hide from it.

CELEBRATE THE WINS

When I decided to follow God's call and pursue vocational ministry, a mentor told me, "You better learn to celebrate the little wins, or you'll never make it." I didn't understand exactly what he meant until I hosted a youth night and five kids showed up. I was gutted. I had all of these grand expectations that fell flat, and before I knew it, the wind had left my sails. That is, until one of the five approached me after the service and said, "I know I'm supposed to read the Bible and I really want to. I just don't know where to start. Can you help me?" Sails officially *re*-winded.

I had to learn how to identify and hold on to wins to avoid frustration and despair. And so, my final encouragement to you and our final element of an outward-focused life is to celebrate every gospel conversation by holding fast to *The Win*.

ASK YOURSELF

- What kind of reactions have I received when sharing my faith in the past?
- What keeps me from pursuing people who have reacted negatively or neutrally?
- How is success measured in evangelism, and how can measuring success correctly lead to celebrating every conversation?

ALWAYS GOING

PUT ME IN, COACH

Not so scary now, is it? Just like the quarterback who's thrown 10,000 passes, studied film each week for thirteen seasons, and taken good care of his body, believers who rightly understand God's mission can't wait to get in the game. It's a beautiful thing when the long hours of practice pay off, but what's even more beautiful is the feeling of confidence that comes from seeing the full picture.

I told you as we began that focusing on the product rather than the journey can make us feel unqualified, ill-equipped, and unworthy. But now that you've put in the practice, don't you feel just a little excited to get out there under the lights?

REGULAR RHYTHMS

When we are rooted in the gospel daily, remember how we've been changed, live lives that glorify God, seek to reach the lost, identify and overcome our fears, understand the part we play in God's mission, labor to reach others lovingly and effectively, and celebrate every gospel conversation, God is faithful to use us.

Each element plays an important part in developing an outward-focused *worldview*, a worldview that leads to an outward-focused *life*. My hope is that you develop a rhythm of cultivating these elements each and every day, calibrating to God's will, His plan, and His mission.

I feel like I should be honest with you about my intentions for writing this book. If you followed along step-by-step, it's possible that you identified some people in your life who need to hear the gospel. Maybe you even shared it with them—and that's fantastic! But here's my confession: I'm actually not after the gospel conversations you might have as a result of reading this little book. I've been to Bible camp too many times to buy into the *spiritual high* that seems life-changing for a few days only to fall flat a week later.

No, I'm after the gospel conversations you'll have fifteen, thirty, forty-five years from now. See, anyone can read a book and do what it says, and any book can say nice things that elicit action from its readers. The real question is whether this book changed your *worldview* and imbued you with ideas that transform the way you think for the rest of your life. Did it give you a new, Christ-centered lens so you can see yourself and others as God sees you? *That* is the question.

ANYONE, ANYTIME, ANYWHERE

The journey doesn't end when you close this book. This is just the beginning. We are invited to begin again and again and again, filling up at the well of God's love and overflowing into others. So, as you turn the page and close the book, do me a favor—flip it over and open it again. Revisit your understanding of the gospel, remember how He changed your heart, examine your lifestyle, and begin the process of reaching the lost all over again.

It's my prayer that through living out these eight simple elements, you will truly be *Always Going*.

ASK YOURSELF

- What images and emotions come to mind when I hear the word *evangelism*?
- On a scale of one to ten, how comfortable do I feel sharing my faith?
- How often do I think about the faith of others?
- Am I ready to get back in the game?

ABOUT ALWAYS GOING

More than just a book, *Always Going* is a ministry dedicated to challenging, equipping, and sending believers to share the gospel. This resource is just one of the many ways we come alongside the church. Through this book, we hope you have seen the heart of *Always Going*—not just evangelistic tips and tricks, but an outward-focused worldview that will have every believer seeking out gospel conversations with anyone, at any time, and anywhere.

We do this through:

- RESOURCES—providing books, curriculum, video series, articles, sermons, and more
- EVENTS— speaking at conferences, breakouts, camps, workshops, Sunday services, or any other church or community event
- LEADER TRAINING—equipping facilitators and teachers to lead others and become part of our nationwide GO Leader network
- CHURCH STRATEGY—helping any local church develop a unique "sending culture" based on its size, denomination, location, priorities, leadership, surrounding community, and any other factors involved

To get involved with *Always Going*, undergo training to lead a group, or bring *Always Going* to your church, reach out to us at www.alwaysgoing.org.